CAMPAIGN 377

SIEGE OF BUDAPEST 1944–45

The Brutal Battle for the Pearl of the Danube

BALÁZS MIHÁLYI

ILLUSTRATED BY JOHNNY SHUMATE

Series editor Nikolai Bogdanovic

OSPREY PUBLISHING
Bloomsbury Publishing Plc
PO Box 883, Oxford, OX1 9PL, UK
29 Earlsfort Terrace, Dublin 2, Ireland
1385 Broadway, 5th Floor, New York, NY 10018, USA
E-mail: info@ospreypublishing.com
www.ospreypublishing.com

OSPREY is a trademark of Osprey Publishing Ltd

First published in Great Britain in 2022

© Osprey Publishing Ltd, 2022

A catalogue record for this book is available from the British Library.

ISBN: PB 9781472848482; eBook 9781472848376;
ePDF 9781472848383; XML 9781472848369

22 23 24 25 26   10 9 8 7 6 5 4 3 2 1

Maps by Bounford.com
3D BEVs by Paul Kime. Note that in this work, the 3D BEVs are based on
modern cartographic mapping of the terrain.
Index by Alan Rutter
Typeset by PDQ Digital Media Solutions, Bungay, UK
Printed and bound in India by Replika Press Private Ltd.

MIX
Paper from
responsible sources
FSC® C016779

Artist's note

Readers can discover more about the work of illustrator Johnny Shumate at
the below website:
https://johnnyshumate.com

Osprey Publishing supports the Woodland Trust, the UK's leading woodland
conservation charity.

To find out more about our authors and books visit
www.ospreypublishing.com. Here you will find extracts, author interviews,
details of forthcoming events and the option to sign up for our newsletter.

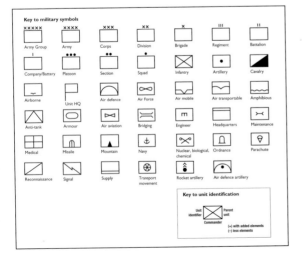

FRONT COVER ILLUSTRATION: The fighting at the Vérmező School,
on the morning of 31 January 1945. (Johnny Shumate)

TITLE PAGE PHOTOGRAPH:
SS artillerymen provide fire support with their 75mm PaK 40
in its camouflaged firing position in Budapest, February 1945.
(Mondadori via Getty Images)

CONTENTS

Operations in the Pannonian Basin, 23 August to 29 October 1944

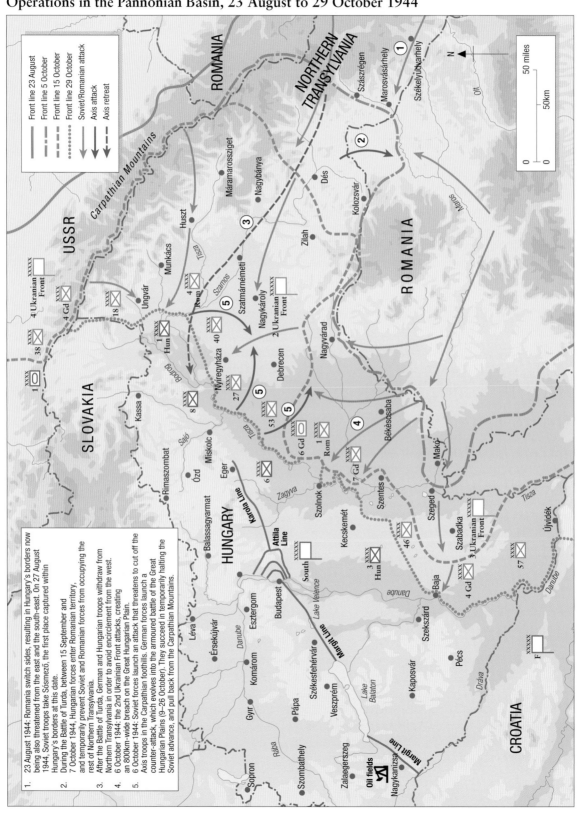

Key:
- Front line 23 August
- Front line 5 October
- Front line 15 October
- Front line 29 October
- Soviet/Romanian attack
- Axis attack
- Axis retreat

1. 23 August 1944: Romania switch sides, resulting in Hungary's borders now being also threatened from the east and the south-east. On 27 August 1944, Soviet troops take Sósmező, the first place captured within Hungary's borders at this date.

2. During the Battle of Turda, between 15 September and 7 October 1944, Hungarian forces enter Romanian territory, and temporarily prevent Soviet and Romanian forces from occupying the rest of Northern Transylvania.

3. After the Battle of Turda, German and Hungarian troops withdraw from Northern Transylvania in order to avoid encirclement from the west.

4. 6 October 1944: the 2nd Ukrainian Front attacks, creating an 800km-wide breach on the Great Hungarian Plain.

5. 6 October 1944: Soviet forces launch an attack that threatens to cut off the Axis troops in the Carpathian foothills. German forces launch a counter-attack, which evolves into the armoured battle of the Great Hungarian Plains (9–26 October). They succeed in temporarily halting the Soviet advance, and pull back from the Carpathian Mountains.

ORIGINS OF THE CAMPAIGN

With the 1938 Anschluss of Austria, German expansion reached Hungary's borders, and the two countries became neighbours. The ensuing period saw the peaceful readjustment of the borders by the First Vienna Award on 2 November 1938, when 12,000km^2 of territory was returned to Hungary.[1] On 30 August 1940, the Second Vienna Award returned a further 43,100km^2 with the reassignment of Northern Transylvania to Hungary. These awards also saw significant ethnic minorities returning under Hungarian rule.

In this period, Hitler did not trust Hungary, nor its military forces – he held Romania, for example, in much higher esteem. Unlike the latter, Hungary did not receive weapons from Germany until 1942. Hitler's resentment was not unfounded, Hungary being something of a reluctant ally. Hungary's interests did not align with Nazi Germany's goals. When Germany invaded Poland, for instance, Hungary refused to allow German troops to cross its territory, and later, at the end of the campaign, Hungary admitted thousands of Polish army personnel, and helped them move to Great Britain, including a significant number of Polish pilots.

In the campaign against Yugoslavia in 1941, Hungary joined Germany just after the dissolution of the Yugoslav state, with its sights set on the Hungarian ethnic groups of the Délvidék. This step, however, meant the loss of Hungary's former neutrality, and Hungary thus entered World War II on the Axis side. In a quick campaign with minimal losses, Hungary occupied and annexed the Délvidék – a territory of 11,600km^2 and a population of 1.1 million, of whom 300,000 were of Hungarian ethnicity.

When Operation *Barbarossa* was launched on 22 June 1941, Hitler did not initially rely on Hungarian support. On 26 June, however, the city of Kassa (modern Košice) was bombed, presumably by Soviet planes, and this resulted in Hungary joining *Barbarossa* by deploying the Hungarian Rapid Corps (*Gyorshadtest*). The Hungarian Army fared poorly against the Red Army, losing all of its light tanks and 80 per cent of its medium tanks. The Rapid Corps reached Donetsk in Ukraine in November 1941, and was subsequently withdrawn. In 1942, the 200,000-strong Hungarian Second Army was sent to the Eastern Front, where it suffered a catastrophic defeat along the Don River in late 1942 and early 1943, and taking 100,000–120,000 casualties.

The Hungarian political regime was well aware that defeat looked likely, and therefore entered ceasefire negotiations with the Western Powers as early as 1942. The country's anti-communist leaders long resisted any negotiations

---

1   Following Austria-Hungary's defeat in World War I, the Treaty of Versailles had resulted in Hungary losing 67 per cent of its territory to Czechoslovakia, Romania, Yugoslavia and, to a lesser extent, Austria.

Romanian infantry photographed near Tápiószentmárton, during their advance towards Budapest. (MTI Photo Archives, FT1919294)

with the Soviet Union. They hoped that by having Anglo-American troops in the Balkans, the country could avoid a Soviet occupation. In 1943, a ceasefire was signed in Istanbul, in essence a preliminary capitulation agreement. With this, Hungary indicated its intentions to capitulate, but intended to keep the agreement secret until Allied forces reached Hungary's borders. Until that point, Hungary undertook to reduce its economic cooperation with Germany, and to withdraw its troops from the Eastern Front.

Germany became aware of Hungary's negotiations, and on 19 March 1944, the country came under German occupation. A pro-German government was installed, yet Miklós Horthy retained his position as regent. By the summer of 1944, as the Red Army approached the Carpathian Mountains, the Hungarian First Army had already been mobilized and deployed in the foothills. On 23 August that year, Romania switched sides and joined the Soviet Union, and Soviet and Romanian troops began to approach from Transylvania. By this time, Horthy had already contacted the Soviet Union to negotiate a ceasefire. This attempt to join the Allies, however, was poorly organized. In his radio address to the nation on 15 October 1944, Horthy called for an uprising against the Germans, but the military did not follow his orders. A significant number of officers were pro-German, and the Hungarian First Army thus did not open the front line to allow the Red Army to pass through.

Prior to this unsuccessful attempt, Horthy had asked the Soviet leadership to halt the forces sent to attack Budapest on the Great Hungarian Plain to allow enough time for Hungarian troops to be rallied around Budapest to support the attempt to switch sides. In line with this, the Soviets did indeed stop their attack, hoping that Hungary would switch, and that the way to Budapest, and then to Vienna, would be opened without a fight. However, on 15 October, with the attempt having failed, the situation changed. Despite Horthy's radio speech, the front line was not opened and the Soviet forces were unable to take Budapest. Germany, on the other hand, reacted immediately, and with Horthy removed, Ferenc Szálasi was put in charge of the country, forming a pro-German government that supported continuing to fight for the Axis, and ordering the military to comply.

The Transdanubia region was of strategic importance to the Germans, with Hitler insisting on its defence primarily for economic reasons. Transdanubia had resources that were deemed vital for German military industry. Following the loss of the Romanian oilfields, Zala held the largest amount of oil, and after the loss of France, Hungarian sources accounted for 90 per cent of the Axis Powers' production of bauxite, a component of the aluminium used in aircraft construction. Both these materials were sourced from the Transdanubia region. For Hitler, the loss of Budapest would mean that the Transdanubia region would also be in danger, and the road to Vienna would lie open. It is no coincidence that Edmund Veesenmayer, Germany's ambassador to Hungary and omnipotent special envoy after the country's German occupation, proclaimed that it did not matter if Budapest was 'destroyed ten times, so long as Vienna could thereby be defended'.

The Soviets saw Budapest as the capital of a potential ally. The city was thus important for them, but following Horthy's unsuccessful attempt, Hungary did not switch sides. This, however, did not diminish Budapest's importance for the Soviets. Budapest's bridges over the Danube, and its industrial facilities, were also of value for the Soviets. Yet, the Soviets overestimated Budapest's significance to German military industry, and they also failed to recognize the strategic importance of Transdanubia's material resources.

After Horthy's unsuccessful attempt, the hope of Hungary switching sides was lost; thus, on 22 December 1944, the Provisional National Government was formed in Debrecen under Soviet rule: it was originally intended to be formed in Budapest, but events did not allow for it at the time. The taking of Budapest would now involve fighting and bloodshed prior to any Soviet occupation – yet this would prove to be a much more difficult undertaking than they would ever have thought.

German troops and a Tiger Ausf. B (King Tiger) in Szent György Square in the Castle, Budapest, at the time of the Arrow Cross seizure of power on 15–16 October 1944. The Arrow Cross Party was a Hungarian nationalist party led by Ferenc Szálasi. (MTI Photo Archives, 752735)

CHRONOLOGY

1944

29 October — Beginning of the Soviet offensive against Budapest.

5 November — German troops launch a counter-attack from the town of Pilis.

22 November — Soviet troops cross the Danube and reach Csepel Island.

1 December — Hitler declares Budapest a fortress city (*Festung*).

5 December — Soviet troops cross the Danube at Ercsi and establish a bridgehead.

22 December — Soviet troops breach the Margit Line and reach the village of Vál.

23 December — Soviet troops take Székesfehérvár.

26 December — Soviet troops take Esztergom and fully surround Budapest.

27 December — The Axis Budapest Supply Corps is established.

1945

1 January — The Germans launch Operation *Konrad I* to relieve Budapest.

3 January — The emergency airfield in Új Lóversenytér Park becomes unusable.

6 January — The airfield on Csepel Island falls within Soviet artillery range and is no longer usable. German troops in Operation *Konrad I* take Esztergom, but the offensive loses momentum.

9 January — Operation *Konrad II* launched.

11 January — German troops from Operation *Konrad II* reach Pilisszentkereszt, only 20km from Budapest, but are halted.

13 January — Soviet troops reach sections of Nagykörút Boulevard in Budapest.

18 January — The Germans evacuate what is left of the Pest bridgehead. The Germans launch Operation *Konrad III* to the south of Lake Velence.

19 January — Operation *Konrad III* forces reach the Danube and surround two Soviet army corps.

22 January — German troops from Operation *Konrad III* take Székesfehérvár. Soviet troops occupy Kis-Sváb Hill in Budapest.

27 January — Operation *Konrad III* is halted.

11–14 February — German and Hungarian breakout attempts from Budapest. Most are killed or captured.

13 February — Buda Castle falls. The siege of Budapest is over.

Hungarian military police on guard at a roadblock in Budapest in December 1944. (MTI Photo Archives, 752848)

OPPOSING COMMANDERS

AXIS

Georg Otto Hermann Balck (1893–1982) served in the German Army from 1913 and fought in World War I, rising to the position of commander of a machine-gun squadron by the end of the war. In 1942, he was given command of the 2nd Armoured Brigade, then of the 11th Panzer Division as major-general. During the defence of Ukraine, his division managed to destroy most of a Soviet tank army, for which he was awarded the Knight's Cross with Oak Leaves, Swords and Diamonds.

In 1943, Balck was given command of Panzer-Grenadier Division Grossdeutschland as a lieutenant-general, and in the same year he was given command of a panzer corps as *General der Panzertruppe*. In August 1944, he was appointed to command Army Group G in France. However, he was unable to stop Patton's advance, and was placed in the officer reserve pool. Then, in December 1944, he assumed control of the reformed German Sixth Army in Hungary. (The former Sixth Army had been destroyed at Stalingrad.)

General Georg Otto Hermann Balck, commander of the German Sixth Army. (ullstein bild via Getty Images)

Gerhard Schmidhuber (1894–1945) enlisted in 1914 as a volunteer in World War I, and was made a reserve lieutenant by 1915. He left the army in 1920. In 1934, he was reactivated, and made a battalion commander in 1939. He fought in the campaigns of Poland and France in the German 4th Infantry Division. In 1941, the latter was reorganized into the 14th Panzer Division, and sent to fight in Yugoslavia, then on the Eastern Front. In September that year, he took command of the 13th Panzer Division, and was promoted to major-general in October. Part of Schmidhuber's division was stuck in the Budapest pocket. During the siege, he also took command of the parts of Panzer Division Feldherrnhalle trapped in Budapest. The northern part of the Pest bridgehead was protected by troops under his command, and in January 1945 he won the Knight's Cross of the Iron Cross with Oak Leaves. Following the abandonment of the Pest bridgehead, he was given control of the southern Buda front line for a short time at the end of the siege. He was killed during the attempted breakout.

Herbert Otto Gille (1897–1966) fought in World War I, and left the army in 1919 as a first lieutenant. He joined the SS in 1940 and fought throughout the French campaign as a battalion commander. In 1941, he took command of a regiment in the 5th SS-Panzer Division Wiking. He also took part in the campaign against the Soviet Union.

In 1943, the Wiking was reorganized into a panzer-grenadier division, and he took command. In 1943, after being surrounded in the Korsun-Cherkassy pocket, he successfully led the division's breakout. In 1944, he relieved and evacuated the German troops surrounded in Kowel, for which he was awarded the Knight's Cross of the Iron Cross with Oak Leaves and Swords. In January 1945, he was given command of the IV SS-Panzer Corps as *SS-Obergruppenführer*, and led the attempts to relieve Budapest in the *Konrad* operations. In March 1945, he led the Lake Balaton offensive. At the end of the war, he was taken prisoner by US forces, and was released in 1948.

Iván Hindy (1890–1946) fought in World War I for Austria-Hungary. A lieutenant by the end of the war, he continued his professional military career in the Royal Hungarian Army. Until 1928, he worked in counter-espionage, then was an instructor at the Ludovika Academy. He was later appointed a department head at the General Command of the Defence Forces, before being reassigned to the Hungarian First Army. On 15 October 1944, he arrested the commander of the Hungarian I Corps, his superior, who wanted to resist the Germans during Horthy's attempt to switch sides. Hindy was subsequently appointed commander of I Corps, and during the siege of Budapest he led the Hungarian troops in the surrounded capital. He was promoted to lieutenant-general during the siege. In the course of the siege, he had no real control as the Germans did not involve him in the planning of military operations, and he was only allowed to conduct supply operations. At the end of the siege, he was taken prisoner by the Soviets, and sentenced to death by the People's Court for his role in the attempted switching of sides. He was executed in 1946.

Johannes Friessner (1892–1971) served in the German Army from 1911, and fought in World War I. After the war, he served in the Reichswehr. He taught tactics at the Dresden military school, and also doubled as an adjutant to the school commander. In 1933, he was promoted to major. From 1938, he served as chief inspector of the military schools in Berlin, and in 1940 he was promoted to major-general. However, due to a falling out with the Nazi Party leadership, he was reassigned to the Eastern Front in 1942, where he took command of the 102nd Infantry Division. The same year, he was also given command of the XXIII Corps. He was promoted to colonel-general in July 1944, and that same month was given command of Army Group South Ukraine (later redesignated Army Group South), which he led until relieved on 22 December 1944. In the armoured battles on the Great Hungarian Plain, he successfully delayed the Soviet advance, and was also successful in holding on to Budapest for a long time. However, he could not prevent the breaching of the Margit Line and the resultant surrounding of Budapest – a fact not condoned by Hitler, who relieved Friessner of command. He was not given any further assignments in the war. Post 1945, he served as president of the German Veterans Association for a time.

Karl Pfeffer-Wildenbruch (1888–1971) was an artillery lieutenant prior to World War I, and served as a battery commander during the war. He was then dispatched as a staff officer to Baghdad, where he served in the Turkish Army. He was sent to Constantinople in 1917 as a member of the German military mission, but returned later that year and became a staff officer in the German 11th Infantry

Colonel-General Johannes Friessner, commander of Army Group South. (ullstein bild via Getty Images)

Division. After the war, he enlisted with the police in 1919 and became a department head in the Ministry of the Interior, overseeing Osnabrück and Magdeburg. Between 1918 and 1930, he served as trainer for the local police forces in Santiago de Chile. He returned to Germany in 1933 and was given command of the Frankfurt police regiment. He enlisted in the SS in 1939. In that year, the Polizei Division was set up, and as the commander of the division, Pfeffer-Wildenbruch took part in the French campaign. The division remained in France as an occupying force and Pfeffer-Wildenbruch rejoined the SS, where he served as a chief of the colonial police until 1943. He then took command of the VI SS-Army Corps on the Eastern Front until June 1944, where he was on the receiving end of the Leningrad–Novgorod Offensive launched by the Soviets. In December 1944, he was appointed commander of the German IX SS-Mountain Corps as an *SS-Obergruppenführer*. This placed him in overall charge of the *Festung* city when Budapest was surrounded. Although he lacked extensive combat experience, particularly of urban warfare at close quarters, his previous experience as a police officer contributed greatly to his appointment. Budapest still retained a large ghetto at the end of 1944, and the Germans were not sure how much resistance to expect from the Hungarian populace. During the siege, he was awarded the Knight's Cross of the Iron Cross with Oak Leaves. Karl Pfeffer-Wildenbruch managed to hold Budapest right to the end. He oversaw military operations from a tunnel under Buda Castle, which he never left until the final breakout. The de facto commander of military operations in practice, however, was the IX SS-Mountain Corps chief of staff, **Lieutenant-Colonel Daniel Maximilian Otto Usdau Lindenau** (1914–84). At the age of 30, Lindenau was one of the youngest corps chiefs in the Wehrmacht. The command of Fortress Budapest was thus in the hands of a police officer with little battlefield experience and a very young, albeit militarily experienced chief of staff, though the division commanders were all veteran soldiers with front experience. At the end of the siege, Pfeffer-Wildenbruch was taken prisoner at the breakout, and was released only in 1955.

SS-Obergruppenführer Karl Pfeffer-Wildenbruch, commander of IX SS-Mountain Corps and later of Fortress Budapest. (ullstein bild via Getty Images)

László Vannay (1898–1945) fought in World War I from beginning to end for Austria-Hungary, before leaving the army as a lieutenant. He helped set up the irregular 'Ragged Guards', and took part in its actions in 1919, then in the irregular fighting on the Austrian border, before serving in the Lajtabánság area on the staff of the Hungarian paramilitary commander Pál Prónay. He was arrested in 1931 for organizing a coup, but was later released. In 1939, he was a leading figure in the Ragged Guards, deployed in irregular operations against Czechoslovakia. In 1939, he was one of the organizers of the Hungarian volunteer force that fought in the Finnish-Soviet Winter War. In October 1944, following the Arrow Cross takeover, he received permission to set up a volunteer detachment, the Vannay Battalion. The battalion remained in the Budapest pocket and defended one of the key sections of the Buda bank of the city until the end of the Városmajor siege. Vannay lost his life in the breakout.

The German command structure in Budapest consisted of numerous parallel lines and was not centralized. Pfeffer-Wildenbruch belonged to the German Sixth Army and, indirectly, to Army Group South. At the same time, Pfeffer-Wildenbruch, as an SS-general, was also a subordinate of Otto Winkelmann, the commander-in-chief of Hungarian SS and police forces.

In addition, he was also a subordinate of Wehrmacht General Hans von Greiffenberg, who was in charge of all German troops in Hungary.

SOVIET AND ROMANIAN

Fedor Ivanovich Tolbukhin (1894–1949) enlisted as a private in World War I, and by the end of the war, he was already a captain in the Russian Army. In 1917, he fought on several fronts. He graduated from the Frunze Military Academy and was appointed to divisional command in 1937. In 1941, he was first made the chief of staff of the Caucasus Front then of the Crimean Front. In 1942, he led the Soviet 57th Army and fought at Stalingrad. In 1943, he took command of the Southern Front, then the 4th and later the 3rd Ukrainian fronts. In 1944, he was promoted to Marshal of the Soviet Union. The 3rd Ukrainian Front took part in the recapture of Crimea and southern Ukraine, in the Iassy-Kishinev Offensive, and in the occupation of Bulgaria and Yugoslavia. In November 1944, Tolbukhin and his troops joined in the military operations against Budapest in the Transdanubia region. He successfully quashed the German *Konrad* operations to relieve Budapest, and following the seizure of Budapest, went on to fight in the offensive to take Vienna. After the war, he first became commander of the Southern Group of Forces, then of the Transcaucasus Military District.

Ivan Mikhailovich Afonin (1904–79) joined the Red Army in 1926 and graduated from the Frunze Military Academy in 1933. In 1939, he fought in the Battle of Khalkhin Gol against the Japanese. In 1941, he was appointed a division commander. After the launch of Operation *Barbarossa*, he fought in the defensive battles along the Soviet–Romanian border. He was wounded and hospitalized in 1942, and on his return, he was appointed commander of the 300th Rifle Division, which fought at Stalingrad. In 1943, he was given command of the 18th Guards Rifle Corps as a major-general. With his troops, he took part in the Battle of Kursk, in the retaking of Kiev, and at Budapest. In the latter operation, he also had command of the Budapest Group, until he was once again wounded. After his recovery, he regained command of the corps in April 1945, and fought in the Manchurian Offensive in July that year. After the war, he served in various corps command roles, and then was an instructor at the Voroshilov Military Academy.

Marshal Fyodor Ivanovich Tolbukhin, commander of the 3rd Ukrainian Front. (Bettmann, via Getty Images)

Ivan Mefodevich Managarov (1898–1981) joined the Russian Army in 1918 and fought in the Civil War. In 1932, he was given command of a Red Army cavalry regiment, and between 1936 and 1938 served in China. He was then given command of the 8th Mounted Division, and from 1941 led first a rifle then a cavalry corps. Between 1943 and the end of the war, he led the Soviet 53rd Army as a lieutenant-general. He fought in the Battle of Kursk, in the operations on the territory of Ukraine, in the Iassy-Kishinev Offensive and in the armoured battles on the Great Hungarian Plain. During the siege of Budapest, with Afonin being wounded, he took control of the Budapest Group. He retired in 1953.

Rodion Yakovlevich Malinovsky (1898–1967) joined the Russian Army in 1914 as a volunteer, and was sent to France in 1916 as a member of the Russian Expeditionary Corps. In 1919, he returned home and joined the Red Army.

In 1941, he was in charge of the 48th Rifle Corps near the Romanian border. In the Battle of Stalingrad, he led the Soviet 2nd Guards Army and prevented Axis forces from relieving the pocket. He fought at Kursk in 1943, then, as the commander of the 2nd Ukrainian Front, he fought in Ukraine. In 1944, in the Iassy-Kishinev Offensive, he crushed the opposing German forces. In September, he was appointed Marshal of the Soviet Union while invading Transylvania and Hungary with his troops. He held negotiations with Miklós Horthy's representatives in Szeged before Horthy's failed attempt to switch sides, after which plans were developed to take Budapest. After the fall of Budapest on 13 February 1945, his front took Bratislava and Vienna, and he then fought in the Manchurian Offensive as the commander of the Transbaikal Front in Mongolia. Until 1947, he headed the Transbaikal-Amur Military District. After Stalin's death, he served as the Commander-in-Chief Soviet Ground Forces from 1953, and then as Minister of Defence from 1957 until his death.

Marshal Rodion Yakovlevich Malinovsky, commander of the 2nd Ukrainian Front. The picture was taken in June 1945. (MTI Photo Archives, 753887)

Nicolae Șova (1885–1966) graduated from military school in 1912, and fought for Romania in the Second Balkan War and World War I. He graduated from the military academy in 1921. In 1931, he was made a regimental commander and then in 1934, was sent to Vienna as a military attaché. He returned to Romania in 1937 and was promoted to brigadier-general. With Ion Antonescu's rise to power, Șova was entrusted with reorganizing Romania's armoured forces, and in 1941, he was given command of the so-called Guard Division, which he led until February 1943. He fought in Operation *Barbarossa* commanding the Guard Division. The division played a key role in the capture of Odessa, and in 1942, he was promoted to major-general. In 1944, with Romania joining the Allies, Șova was given command of the Romanian VII Corps. On the Soviet side, he fought in the battles on the Great Hungarian Plain, in the crossing of the Tisza and in the siege of Budapest until his troops were withdrawn. He protested against this withdrawal, and was relieved shortly thereafter. He was arrested in 1946, and two years later was sentenced to 10 years imprisonment for his role in Antonescu's government. He was released from prison in 1956.

The two Soviet marshals, Tolbukhin and Malinovsky, had similar early military careers, and both gained significant wartime experience in major battles – yet both lacked experience of urban warfare. At Stalingrad, neither took part in the military operations within the city limits. Afonin, on the other hand, did have such experience. The planning for the Budapest offensive was placed in Malinovsky's hands, but events quickly diverged from them, and he had to modify and re-plan the operations again and again. Tolbukhin's troops were initially sent to the area as a relief force, and though he did not succeed in keeping to the plans to take the city, his foiling of the German relief attempts can be considered a significant success.

The Soviet command structure in taking Budapest was far from centralized. The 2nd and 3rd Ukrainian fronts operated independently. For the 2nd Ukrainian Front, the 'Budapest Group' was established to coordinate the taking of the capital. However, the mandate of the group was limited to the 2nd Ukrainian Front, and moreover, the staff of the 18th Guards Rifle Corps were assigned this task – something well beyond the usual duties of a corps staff.

OPPOSING FORCES

AXIS

Infantry and artillery

The Siege of Budapest was rather particular in that urban warfare is predominantly an infantry and artillery task, yet the Germans had no infantry divisions in Budapest; only SS cavalry divisions, panzer divisions and elements of a panzer-grenadier division were located there.

The 8th SS-Cavalry Division Florian Geyer consisted of three SS cavalry regiments, an SS artillery regiment, an SS AA artillery battalion, an SS armoured reconnaissance battalion, an SS AT battalion, and an SS pioneer battalion. The cavalry regiments consisted of four cavalry squadrons, a mortar squadron and a heavy weapons squadron.

By late December 1944, however, the numbers of troops and weapons in the two SS-cavalry divisions dropped considerably. Around 25 December, 8th SS-Cavalry Division numbered around 8,000 troops, with its fighting strength only a fraction thereof. Already on 16 December, the fighting strength of the cavalry regiments totalled 900, and that of the armoured reconnaissance battalion was 400 troops.

The 22nd SS-Volunteer Cavalry Division Maria Theresia also included an SS assault gun battalion, in contrast to the other SS mounted division. Its strength stood at about 11,000 troops by late December 1944. While the 8th SS-Cavalry Division had extensive experience of fighting on the Eastern Front, in contrast the 22nd SS-Volunteer Cavalry Division had barely any experience by the time Budapest was surrounded. This division consisted of troops recruited from ethnic Germans living in Hungary and Transylvania, and they had not completed bootcamp by the time they were deployed in southern Pest. These two units represented the strongest German forces in Budapest. Besides these two, not including the panzer divisions, only two grenadier regiments (977th and 978th) of the 271st Volks-Grenadier Division, and the German 1st SS-Police Regiment, remained in the city, totalling a few thousand troops.

On the German side, in the absence of infantry troops, the defensive battles of the siege were fought by mounted troops, AT grenadiers and AA artillery personnel. The role Hungarian forces played in protecting the city was therefore significant. The defence relied heavily on the field fortifications of the partially built Attila Line, at the Pest bridgehead, then on the defensive zones established within the city. The defenders took advantage of natural and artificial cover, and insufficient staffing was made up for with extra firepower. They were able to use their machine guns and carbines to keep the streets under suppressive fire. The standard procedure to counter Soviet incursions was to carry out counter-attacks backed up by armoured units. Later, to further support these manoeuvres, reserve groups of up to 200 troops each were established behind the front line, to be deployed to counter Soviet incursions in the most exposed sections. Infantry battles were supported by artillery; however, due to ammunition shortages, restrictions were quickly introduced on its use (including daily limits), and artillery was allowed to fire only at specific targets. Ammunition took up the greatest volume of supplies brought into the city, and artillery ammunition was by far in the greatest demand.

Armour

Two German panzer divisions were stranded in the Budapest pocket, neither at full strength. In late December 1944, the total headcount of the 13th Panzer Division in Budapest stood at 4,983 troops, and included the 4th Panzer Regiment, the 66th and the 93rd Panzer-Grenadier regiments, the 13th Panzer Artillery Regiment, the 13th Armoured Reconnaissance Battalion and the 4th Armoured Pioneer Battalion.

The headcount of Panzer-Grenadier Division Feldherrnhalle's Budapest force stood at 7,255 troops, and it included Panzer Regiment Feldherrnhalle, the Panzer-Grenadier Regiment Feldherrnhalle, the Panzer Artillery Regiment Feldherrnhalle, the Armoured Anti-Aircraft Artillery Battalion Feldherrnhalle, the Anti-Tank Battalion Feldherrnhalle, the Armoured Reconnaissance Group Feldherrnhalle and the Armoured Pioneer Battalion Feldherrnhalle.[2]

Previous experience (at Stalingrad, for instance) taught the Germans that using panzer units in urban combat was impractical, but now a significant armoured force was trapped in the Budapest pocket. Fuel shortage severely limited their ability to deploy. In urban battles, the panzers were employed individually or in small groups, stopping Soviet attacks and forcing them to deal with tanks one by one. Overall, however, tanks played only a subordinate role in the defence of the Hungarian capital compared to infantry and artillery. From the German side, a total of 38 tanks (including more than a dozen PzKpfw V Panthers), 38 panzerjäger and 13 assault guns (Stug III and M42 Semovente units), as well as 23 self-propelled (SP) guns (mostly Hummel units) were trapped in Budapest.

An abandoned Panzer IV on the Pest side of the city. At the beginning of 1945, the German 3rd Panzer Division had a total of 102 tanks, assault guns and panzerjägers, including 47 PzKpfw V Panthers; the German 6th Panzer Division had 68 tanks, assault guns and panzerjägers, including 32 PzKpfw V Panther units; and the German 8th Panzer Division had 72 tanks, assault guns and panzerjägers, including 42 PzKpfw V Panther units. (MTI Photo Archives, 753118)

Air supremacy played a pivotal role in German panzer tactics on the Eastern Front, but now it was less and less feasible. German armour was most successful in defensive actions when Soviet offensive forces managed to reach deep behind the lines, where they could be attacked from the side, as happened during the first Soviet attack on Budapest. However, without air supremacy, attacks on Soviet defensive

2 Panzer-Grenadier Division Feldherrnhalle was renamed Panzer Division Feldherrnhalle on 27 November 1944.

positions proved to be more and more difficult compared to what had been the case during *Konrad I*. Infantry support to armoured units was also crucial, as without this the panzers were unable to successfully breach the lines – as demonstrated during Operation *Konrad III*.

Aviation

By late 1944, the Luftwaffe no longer possessed the necessary air strength to gain anything more than transient air superiority in this sector. German fighters rarely managed to cover the skies over Budapest, and thus aerial transports suffered heavy losses; daytime operations had to be abandoned after a while, with flights limited only to nighttime. Fighters, fighter-bombers and strike aircraft were deployed primarily to support the *Konrad* relief operations.

At the end of 1944, the German 4th Air Fleet consisted of 131 Bf 109 fighters, 141 Fw 190 fighter-bombers, 46 Ju 87 dive-bombers, 27 Hs 129 strike aircraft, 80 He 111 bombers, 67 Ju 52 transport aircraft, and 45 Go 145 and 20 Ar 66 night-fighters.

Hungarian forces

By the end of October 1944, the Hungarian infantry divisions were already in a weakened state: the 8th Infantry Division had a fighting force of 3,300, the 10th Infantry Division 800, the 20th Infantry Division 1,500, the 23rd Reserve Division 3,600, and the Hungarian 1st Cavalry Division 3,700.

By late December 1944, the strength of the Hungarian forces trapped in Budapest surpassed that of the Germans (51,000 vs 45,000), but in terms of fighting strength they were inferior (out of a total 15,000 combatants, only 5,000 were Hungarian). However, the role of Hungarian forces was essential to the success of defending Budapest. At this date, the 10th Infantry Division had fewer than 1,000 combatants out of a total headcount of *c*. 7,500, and the 12th Reserve Division had around 1,200 combatants out of 4,000 in total. Beyond these two divisions, the most significant units were the 1st Armoured Division (5,000 personnel), the elements of the 1st Cavalry Division (*c*. 1,000 troops), the Assault Artillery divisions (around 2,000 strong), the Budapest Guard Battalion (800 troops), the Vannay Battalion (638 troops), the Academy Assault battalions (totalling 1,000), and the five Gendarme battalions (3,000 in total). The Hungarian police and various makeshift battle groups were deployed at the bridgehead, but their numbers did not exceed 2,000 in either case. The majority of AA artillery at the bridgehead was also provided by Hungarian forces with 130 AA guns (Hungarian 8cm and German 8.8cm guns, as well as 85mm guns captured from the Soviets) and 100 AA machine guns.

Hungarian small arms comprised 7.92mm 35M and 7.92mm 43M repeating rifles, 9mm Király (39M, 43M) submachine guns, 8mm Solothurn (31M) light machine guns, and 20mm Solothurn (36M) AT rifles. The Hungarian-developed 44M Buzogányvető anti-infantry missile, used in the siege of Budapest, is also worth mentioning.

The Hungarian Assault Artillery battalions had 14 Zrínyi assault howitzers and 16 Turán tanks, both of Hungarian design. In mid-December 1944, the Hungarian 1st Armoured Division had two Turán tanks, three Toldi tanks and five Nimród AA guns, all of Hungarian design. The gendarmes deployed in Budapest also had five Ansaldo mini tanks of Italian design.

SOVIET AND ROMANIAN

Infantry and artillery

At the beginning of 1945, a total of 165,000 Soviet troops were involved in the battle for Budapest. Of these, 85,000 attacked the Pest bank of the Danube and 80,000 the Buda side. In terms of artillery, 160 AT guns, 887 artillery pieces and 48 rocket launchers were used in Pest, and 188 AT guns, 744 artillery guns and 140 rocket launchers in Buda.

As per 1943 organization, a Soviet rifle division's strength was set at 9,380 troops. A rifle division consisted of the division staff, three rifle regiments, an artillery regiment and an AT artillery division. The division also had a signals and a reconnaissance company, and a machine-gun and an engineer battalion.

In practice, however, the actual headcount of a rifle division was much lower – during the siege of Budapest, sometimes less than half the requirement. Another problem was that Hungary was considered a secondary theatre of operations in terms of both manpower and equipment supply, deficiencies that were hard to make up for. It was no coincidence then that, by the end of the siege, penal units and Hungarian volunteers defecting to the Soviets were also deployed. Out of all the Hungarian corps established in Soviet-occupied territories during the war, only the Hungarian companies established in Buda were actually deployed to fight against the Germans.

With the exception of Stalingrad, the Red Army lacked opportunities to gain extensive urban warfare experience until 1944. Based on the former, at Budapest the Soviets organized assault groups within rifle divisions. These included riflemen, engineers, gunners and also tank crews on occasion. Each assault group had two subgroups, an attack one and a blocking one. The attack subgroup was tasked with entering the objective to be occupied, while the blocking subgroup made sure that the objective remained isolated and unable to receive outside help.

When attacking, the engineers would dismantle or clear paths through or around any obstacles (such as minefields), and blow up barricades or holes through walls, opening a path for the attackers. Artillery was tasked with suppressing resistance hotspots, camouflaged guns and emplacements through direct fire. The attack subgroup riflemen would then enter the building, while the blocking subgroup would secure it from the outside. Anti-aircraft machine guns were deployed against enemy infantry. The attacking subgroup would try to reach and clear the top level of the buildings first, then squeeze out the defenders from the top down. Soviet forces tried to seize every opportunity to occupy housing blocks – even using the underground system of air-raid shelters. They also attacked through the roofs to the same effect, but they did not manage to take advantage of the sewer network.

The size of assault groups varied from between 15 and 20 to 50 troops, depending on the target. In terms

A still from the Soviet movie *The Siege of Budapest*, showing Soviet 152mm howitzers preparing to rain group fire on the city in late December 1944. (MTI Photo Archives, 754345)

of armament, riflemen were equipped with submachine guns, and were supported by light machine guns, AT guns, flamethrowers and direct-fire guns of various calibre, and sometimes AA machine guns and even tanks.

When rifle divisions had to move to the defensive, they established so-called AT zones where they concentrated various AT items equipment (45mm and 76mm AT guns, 14.5cm AT rifles). Anti-tank zones were generally established in three lines in depth, at battalion, regiment and division levels. At the division level, 122mm and sometimes 152mm guns were also emplaced for direct-fire AT tasks. This tactic was also successfully used throughout the *Konrad* operations, supplemented by the laying of AT mines and the placement of tanks in ambush positions. Such AT zones were camouflaged as best they could be. A weak point in the armament of the rifle divisions was the lack of AA weaponry, and riflemen did not have bazookas (unlike the Germans). Thus, by 1944, they only had obsolete 14.5cm AT rifles, which were no longer effective against German tanks. Because of this, they had to use Molotov cocktails and AT grenades.

Armour

A model Soviet tank corps had a strength of 11,636 troops, and consisted of three tank brigades, a truck-mounted rifle brigade and the artillery regiments. The tank brigades consisted of three tank battalions and a truck-mounted rifle battalion, as well as an AT battery and an AA machine-gun squadron.

A tank corps had 207 T-34 tanks, 21 Su-76 SP guns, 21 Su-85 or Su-100 SP guns, 21 ISU-122 or ISU-152 SP guns, 23 BA-64 armoured vehicles, and small arms comprising 4,741 rifles, 3,725 submachine guns, 243 shotguns, 57 machine guns, 52 heavy rifles and 203 AT rifles (14.5cm). It also had 52 82mm and 42 120mm mortars, 12 45mm and four 57mm AT guns, 68 76mm guns, and an M-13 rocket battery. A Soviet Mechanized corps had a set strength of 16,753 troops, and consisted of three mechanized brigades, a tank brigade and artillery regiments.

Soviet mechanized and tank corps still followed the operational doctrine developed in the 1930s, which focused on deep breaches through the enemy lines. This was accomplished by engaging the front line, breaching it at a selected point then penetrating it in great depth. In the assault stage, the rifle corps, accompanied by tanks and artillery, breached the defences. In the successive development stage, fast-moving mechanized, mounted and tank corps penetrated behind the enemy's lines, and tried to advance deep into enemy territory, but this was often a risky manoeuvre due to the flanks of the advancing forces being undefended.

In the battles within Budapest, the Soviets used only a limited number of tanks, and only for specific tasks. This was because the battlefield was not easy to oversee, and tanks were easily destroyed in ambushes. Tanks thus played a subordinate role within the urban fighting, supporting the infantry and the artillery.

A still from the Soviet movie *The Siege of Budapest*, with Soviet T-34 tanks advancing towards Budapest. (MTI Photo Archives, 754343)

At the end of October 1944, as an example, the 2nd Guards Mechanized Corps had a strength of 16,000 troops, armed with 185 T-34 and 21 IS-2 tanks, and 21 Su-85 and 21 Su-76 SP guns. The 4th Guards Mechanized Corps was weaker in strength, with 13,000 troops, 109 T-34 tanks, and eight Su-85 and 14 Su-122 SP guns.

At the start of 1945, Soviet operations within Budapest were supported by 30 T-34 tanks and 11 SP guns in Pest, and 38 tanks (mainly T-34s) and 48 SP guns in Buda. During the German relief attempts in January 1945, the Soviet 23rd Tank Corps had a strength of 10,000 troops and 153 T-34 tanks.

This still from the Soviet movie *The Siege of Budapest* shows a group of A-20 Boston light bombers over the Hungarian capital. (MTI Photo Archives, 754342)

Aviation

The primary task of the Soviet military air forces was to support their ground troops. At the end of 1944, the Soviet 5th Air Army had a strength of 139 Yak-1, six Yak-3, 28 Yak-7, 21 Yak-9, 137 La-5 and two La-7 fighters, 185 Il-2 strike aircraft, 75 Douglas A-20 Boston light bombers and 54 Po-2 biplanes. The Soviet 17th Air Army comprised 247 Yak-1 and 221 La-5 fighters, 380 Il-2 strike aircraft, 10 Boston Mk III light bombers and a single Po-2 biplane at the end of 1944.

Air support played an important role in Soviet deep-breach tactics, as well as in urban combat, and Soviet planes were difficult to counter from ground level. Yet, here too the fragmented nature of the Soviet leadership became apparent as the siege lengthened. Malinovsky was initially confident that Budapest would be taken promptly, and did not rely on air support, whereas Tolbukhin, though also optimistic, used the 17th Air Army from the outset. With the launch of the *Konrad* operations, however, the 17th Air Army was deployed against German relief forces, and supporting the battles within the city was left to the Soviet 5th Air Army primarily. As a result, one of the strike aircraft corps was relocated to Ferihegy Airport, and was thus able to deploy from only a short distance away. In the urban fighting, Il-2 strike aircraft provided the greatest support, serving as airborne artillery. However, the winter weather severely limited air operations, with sorties impossible on many days.

Troops of the Romanian 2nd Infantry Division manning positions on the outskirts of Budapest. Romanian small arms included 7.92mm 1924 M ZB carbines, 7.92mm 1930 ZB machine guns, 7.95mm Mannlicher M1895 rifles, 7.62mm Mosin-Nagant M1891 and M1891/30 rifles and 9mm Orita M1941 submachine guns. (Sovfoto/Universal Images Group via Getty Images)

Romanian forces

The Romanian VII Corps consisted of the 2nd and 19th Infantry divisions and the 9th Cavalry Division, with a total strength of 36,000 troops. Romanian troops played a secondary role in the siege, subordinate to the Soviets.

ORDERS OF BATTLE

DANUBE–TISZA AREA, 31 OCTOBER 1944

Listed below are opposing forces present in the Danube–Tisza interfluve, and along the Tisza River, on 31 October 1944.

GERMAN/HUNGARIAN

(Unless otherwise indicated, all units are German formations.)
Army Group South (Colonel-General Johannes Friessner)
Hungarian Third Army (Lieutenant-General József Heszlényi)
  Hungarian VIII Army Corps (Lieutenant-General Béla Lengyel)
    Hungarian 1st Cavalry Division
    Hungarian 5th Replacement Division
    Hungarian 8th Replacement Division
    Hungarian 20th Infantry Division
  LVII Panzer Corps (Lieutenant-General Friedrich Kirchner)
    Hungarian 1st Armoured Division
    23rd Panzer Division
    24th Panzer Division
Sixth Army (Fretter-Pico Army Group) (Artillery General Maximilian Fretter-Pico)
  Hungarian II Army Corps (Lieutenant-General István Kiss)
    Hungarian 12th Reserve Division
    Hungarian 8th Infantry Division
  LXXII Army Corps (Lieutenant-General August Schmidt)
    76th Infantry Division
  IV Panzer Corps (Panzer General Ulrich Kleemann)
    4th SS-Police Panzer-Grenadier Division
  Army troops
    Panzer-Grenadier Division Feldherrnhalle
    1st Panzer Division
    22nd SS-Volunteer Cavalry Division
4th Air Fleet (Lieutenant-General Otto Dessloch)
  10th Squadron, 2nd Anti-Tank Group (Ju 87)
  4th Squadron, 2nd Night Assault Aviation Group (Ju 87)
  I./2nd Assault Aviation Wing (Fw 190)
  II./2nd Assault Aviation Wing (Fw 190)
  III./2nd Assault Aviation Wing (Ju 87)
  I./4th Bomber Aviation Wing (He 111)
  II./4th Bomber Aviation Wing (He 111)
  5th Night Assault Aviation Group (Ju 87)
  14th Squadron, 9th Anti-Tank Group (Hs 129)
  10th Night Assault Aviation Group (Ju 87)
  I./10th Assault Aviation Wing (Fw 190)
  II./10th Assault Aviation Wing (Fw 190)
  III./10th Assault Aviation Wing (Fw 190)
  II./100th Night Fighter Aviation Wing (Ju 88)
  2nd Squadron, 12th Close Range Reconnaissance Aviation Group (Bf 109)
  14th Close Range Reconnaissance Aviation Group (Bf 109)
  II./51st Fighter Aviation Wing (Bf 109)
  II./52nd Fighter Aviation Wing (Bf 109)
  II./53rd Fighter Aviation Wing (Bf 109)
  102nd Aviation Wing (Hungarian)
    1st Squadron, 101st Fighter Aviation Group (Bf 109)
    2nd Squadron, 101st Fighter Aviation Group (Bf 109)
    102nd Close Range Reconnaissance Aviation Squadron (Ju 88)
    102nd Long Range Reconnaissance Aviation Squadron (Fw 189)
    1st Squadron, 102nd High Speed Bomber Aviation Group (Me 210)
    2nd Squadron, 102nd High Speed Bomber Aviation Group (Me 210)
    1st Squadron, 102nd Assault Aviation Group (Fw 190)

SOVIET/ROMANIAN

(Unless otherwise indicated, all units are Red Army formations.)
2nd Ukrainian Front (Marshal Rodion Yakovlevich Malinovsky)
7th Guards Army (Major-General Mikhail Stepanovich Shumilov)
  24th Guards Rifle Corps (Major-General Peter Avdeyenko)
    72nd Guards Rifle Division
    81st Guards Rifle Division
  25th Guards Rifle Corps (Major-General Ganiy Safiulin)
    36th Guards Rifle Division
    53rd Rifle Division
    297th Rifle Division
  27th Guards Rifle Corps (Major-General Yevgeniy Alechin)
    227th Rifle Division
    303rd Rifle Division
  Army troops
    409th Guards Rifle Division
  Romanian First Army (subordinate to the 7th Guards Army) (Lieutenant-General Nicolae Macici)
    Romanian IV Army Corps (Major-General Nicolae Scariat Stoenescu)
      Romanian 2nd Infantry Division
      Romanian 4th Infantry Division
    Romanian VII Army Corps (Major-General Nicolae Sova)
      Romanian 19th Infantry Division
      Romanian 4th Cavalry Division
46th Army (Lieutenant-General Ivan Timofeevich Shlemin)
  10th Guards Rifle Corps (Lieutenant-General Ivan A. Rubanyuk)
    49th Guards Rifle Division
    86th Guards Rifle Division
    109th Guards Rifle Division
  31st Guards Rifle Corps (Major-General Sergey Antonovich Bobruk)
    34th Guards Rifle Division
    40th Guards Rifle Division
  23rd Rifle Corps (Major-General Mikhail Grigorovich)
    68th Guards Rifle Division
    99th Rifle Division
    316th Rifle Division
  37th Rifle Corps (Major-General Fyodor Kolchuk)
    59th Guards Rifle Division
    108th Guards Rifle Division
    320th Rifle Division
  2nd Guards Mechanized Corps (Major-General Karp Vailevich Sviridov)
    4th Guards Mechanized Brigade
    5th Guards Mechanized Brigade
    6th Guards Mechanized Brigade
    37th Tank Brigade
  4th Guards Mechanized Corps (Lieutenant-General Vladimir Zhdanov)
    13th Guards Mechanized Brigade
    14th Guards Mechanized Brigade
    15th Guards Mechanized Brigade
    36th Tank Brigade
  Army troops
    4th Guards Rifle Division
5th Air Army (Lieutenant-General Sergey Goryunov)
  218th Bomber Aviation Division (A-20 Boston)
  312th Night Bomber Aviation Division (Po-2)
  3rd Guards Fighter Aviation Corps (Lieutenant-General Ivan Podgorny)
    6th Guards Fighter Aviation Division (Yak)
    13th Guards Fighter Aviation Division (Yak, La-5)
    14th Guards Fighter Aviation Division (La-5)
  3rd Guards Assault Aviation Corps (Lieutenant-General Vasiliy Stepichev)

7th Guards Assault Aviation Division (Il-2)
12th Guards Assault Aviation Division (Il-2)
279th Fighter Aviation Division (La-5)
5th Assault Aviation Corps (Major-General Nikolai Kamanin)
4th Guards Assault Aviation Division (Il-2)
264th Assault Aviation Division (Il-2)
331st Fighter Aviation Division (Yak-1, Yak-9)

LAKE BALATON–DANUBE/ BUDAPEST AREA, 1 JANUARY 1945

Listed below are opposing forces present in the area between Lake Balaton and the Danube, and in the vicinity of Budapest, on 1 January 1945

GERMAN/HUNGARIAN

(Unless otherwise indicated, all units are German formations.)
Army Group South (Colonel-General Johannes Friessner)
Hungarian Third Army (Colonel-General József Heszlényi)
Hungarian II Army Corps (Major-General István Kiss)
Hungarian 25th Infantry Division
Sixth Army (Panzer General Georg Otto Hermann Balck)
Breith Group (Panzer General Hermann Albert Breith)
III Panzer Corps (only the Corps Staff) (Panzer General Hermann Albert Breith)
Cavalry Corps (Cavalry General Gustav Harteneck)
1st Panzer Division
23rd Panzer Division
4th Cavalry Brigade
Pape Group (Major-General Günther Pape)
3rd Panzer Division
6th Panzer Division
8th Panzer Division
271st Volks-Grenadier Division (elements)
Hungarian 1st Cavalry Division (elements) (Colonel Zoltán Schell)
Hungarian VIII Army Corps (Lieutenant-General Béla Lengyel)
Hungarian 20th Infantry Division (Major-General Jenő Tömöry)
IX SS-Mountain Corps (SS-Obergruppenführer Karl Pfeffer-Wildenbruch)
Hungarian I Corps (subordinated to IX SS-Mountain Corps) (Lieutenant-General Iván Hindy)
Panzer Division Feldherrnhalle (Major-General Gerhard Schmidhuber)
8th SS-Cavalry Division (SS-Brigadeführer Joachim Rumohr)
13th Panzer Division (Major-General Gerhard Schmidhuber)
22nd SS-Volunteer Cavalry Division (SS-Brigadeführer August Zehender)
271st Volks-Grenadier Division (elements) (Major Herbert Kündiger)
Hungarian 1st Cavalry Division (elements)
Hungarian 1st Armoured Division (Colonel János Vértessy)
Hungarian 10th Infantry Division (Colonel Sándor András)
Hungarian 12th Reserve Division (Major-General István Baumann)
Hungarian Assault Artillery Division (Major-General Ernő Billnitzer)
Hungarian 23rd Reserve Division (outside of Budapest)
Directly subordinated to Army Group South:
IV SS-Panzer Corps (SS-Obergruppenführer Herbert Otto Gille)
3rd SS-Panzer Division
5th SS-Panzer Division
96th Infantry Division
711th Infantry Division
4th Air Fleet (Lieutenant-General Otto Dessloch)
2nd Squadron, 10th Assault Aviation Group (Ju 87, Ju 88)
2nd Squadron, 4th Night Assault Aviation Group (Go 145, Ar 66)

I./2nd Assault Aviation Wing (Fw 190)
II./2nd Assault Aviation Wing (Fw 190)
III./2nd Assault Aviation Wing (Ju 87)
I./4th Bomber Aviation Wing (He 111)
II./4th Bomber Aviation Wing (He 111)
III./4th Bomber Aviation Wing (He 111)
5th Night Assault Aviation Group (Go 145, Ar 66)
9th Squadron, 10th Assault Aviation Group (Hs 129)
14th Squadron, 9th Assault Aviation Group (Hs 129)
I./10th Assault Aviation Wing (Fw 190)
II./10th Assault Aviation Wing (Fw 190)
III./10th Assault Aviation Wing (Fw 190)
12th Squadron, 2nd Close Range Reconnaissance Aviation Group (Bf 109)
14th Close Range Reconnaissance Aviation Group (Bf 109)
16th Squadron, 2nd Close Range Reconnaissance Aviation Group (Fw 189)
II./51st Fighter Aviation Wing (Bf 109)
II./52nd Fighter Aviation Wing (Bf 109)
II./53rd Fighter Aviation Wing (Bf 109)
3rd Squadron, 121st Reconnaissance Aviation Group (Ju 188)
Budapest Supply Staff (Lieutenant-General Gerhard Conrad)
III./2nd Transport Aviation Group (Ju 52)
III./3rd Transport Aviation Group (Ju 52)
Hungarian 1st Squadron, 102nd Transport Group (Ju 52)
Hungarian 2nd Squadron, 102nd Transport Group (Ju 52)

SOVIET/ROMANIAN

(Unless otherwise indicated, all units are Red Army formations.)
3rd Ukrainian Front (Marshal Fyodor Ivanovich Tolbukhin)
4th Army (Lieutenant-General Ivan Timofeevich Shlemin)
10th Guards Rifle Corps (Lieutenant-General Ivan A. Rubanyuk)
49th Guards Rifle Division
86th Guards Rifle Division
109th Guards Rifle Division
108th Rifle Division
23rd Rifle Corps (Major-General Mikhail Grigorovich)
99th Rifle Division
316th Rifle Division
83rd Naval Infantry Brigade
37th Rifle Corps (Major-General Fyodor Kolchuk)
59th Guards Rifle Division
108th Guards Rifle Division
320th Rifle Division
4th Guards Army
20th Guards Rifle Corps (Lieutenant-General Nikolay Mikhailovich Dreier)
5th Guards Airborne Division
7th Guards Airborne Division
80th Guards Rifle Division
21st Guards Rifle Corps (Major-General Fyodorov Vasiliy Petrovich)
62nd Guards Rifle Division
69th Guards Rifle Division
31st Guards Rifle Corps (Major-General Sergey Antonovich Bobruk)
4th Guards Rifle Division
34th Guards Rifle Division
40th Guards Rifle Division
68th Rifle Corps (Major-General Ivan Mikhailovich Nekrasov)
52nd Rifle Division
93rd Rifle Division
223rd Rifle Division
135th Rifle Corps
41st Guards Rifle Division
84th Rifle Division
252nd Rifle Division
Directly subordinated to 3rd Ukrainian Front:
1st Guards Mechanized Corps (Major-General Ivan Nikitich Russiyanov)

1st Guards Mechanized Rifle Brigade
2nd Guards Mechanized Rifle Brigade
3rd Guards Mechanized Rifle Brigade
3rd Guards Tank Brigade
2nd Guards Mechanized Corps (Major-General Karp Vailevich Sviridov)
4th Guards Mechanized Rifle Brigade
5th Guards Mechanized Rifle Brigade
6th Guards Mechanized Rifle Brigade
37th Guards Tank Brigade
5th Guards Cavalry Corps (Major-General Alexey Ivanovich Dutkin)
11th Guards Cavalry Division
12th Guards Cavalry Division
63rd Cavalry Division
7th Mechanized Corps (Major-General Fyodor Grigoryevich Katkov)
16th Guards Mechanized Brigade
63rd Guards Mechanized Brigade
64th Guards Mechanized Brigade
41st Guards Tank Brigade
18th Tank Corps (Major-General Petr Dmitrievich Govorunenko)
110th Tank Brigade
170th Tank Brigade
181th Tank Brigade
32nd Mechanized Rifle Brigade
17th Air Army (Lieutenant-General Vladimir Alexandrovich Sudets)
10th Assault Aviation Corps (Lieutenant-General Oleg Viktorovich Tolstikov)
136th Assault Aviation Division
189th Assault Aviation Division
306th Assault Aviation Division
224th Bomber Aviation Division
194 Fighter Aviation Division
288th Fighter Aviation Division
295th Fighter Aviation Division
262nd Night Bomber Aviation Division

2nd Ukrainian Front (Marshal Rodion Yakovlevich Malinovsky)
7th Guards Army (Major-General Mikhail Stepanovich Shumilov)
30th Rifle Corps (Major-General Grigory Lazko)
25th Guards Rifle Division
151st Rifle Division
155st Rifle Division
Romanian VII Army Corps (Major-General Nicolae Sova)
Romanian 2nd Infantry Division
Romanian 9th Cavalry Division
Romanian 19th Infantry Division
Directly subordinated to 2nd Ukrainian Front:
18th Guards Rifle Corps (Major-General Ivan Mikhailovich Afonin)
66th Rifle Division
68th Rifle Division
297th Rifle Division
317th Rifle Division
5th Air Army (Colonel-General Sergei Kondratyevich Goryunov)
3rd Guards Fighter Aviation Corps (Major-General Podgorny Ivan Dmitrievich)
13th Guards Fighter Aviation Division
14th Guards Fighter Aviation Division
3rd Guards Assault Aviation Corps (Lieutenant-General Vasily Vasilievich Stepichev)
7th Guards Assault Aviation Division
12th Guards Assault Aviation Division
5th Assault Aviation Corps (Major-General Nikolai Petrovich Kamanin)
4th Guards Assault Aviation Division
264th Guards Assault Aviation Division
331st Fighter Aviation Division
6th Guards Fighter Aviation Division
279th Fighter Aviation Division
218th Bomber Aviation Division
312th Night Bomber Aviation Division

Civilian prisoners of war on the march through Budapest. During and after the siege, nearly 90,000 civilians (including women) were taken to the Soviet Union as prisoners of war, and a significant number never returned. (MTI Photo Archives, 752900)

OPPOSING PLANS

AXIS

The construction of a defensive line around Budapest, the so-called Attila Line, had already begun in September 1944. At the heart of this was an AT ditch, supplemented with additional obstacles (minefields, anti-infantry wire barriers, etc.) as well as infantry trenches and earth and wood entrenchments. In addition, artillery emplacements were also created to cover the AT ditch.

The Attila Line was not one, but three separate lines separated by their depth (the Attila I, Attila II and Attila III lines), and though not completed by the time of the siege, it still proved to be of significant help to the defenders. For instance, in the Gödöllő Hills, only the valleys were closed off, and barriers were not used on the wooded hillsides because the terrain was unsuitable for tanks. At the same time, the installation of fortified strongpoints also began in Pest, and six more defensive lines were established on the Pest side within the city.

The Attila Line was connected to the Margit Line, of similar design, between Lake Balaton and Budapest, and to the Karola Line in the gap between the Mátra and Zemplén mountain ranges. With this, these three lines formed an almost entirely closed defensive system. After Horthy's unsuccessful attempt to change sides, and as a result of the Debrecen tank battle, which required reinforcement troops to be redirected to the Great Hungarian Plain on 25 October, only the German 22nd SS-Volunteer Cavalry Division, smaller Hungarian units and Hungarian AA artillery were available to man these positions.

A German Hummel SP gun in the Tabán district of Buda, in front of Alexandriai Szent Katalin Parish Church. (Fortepan, 175187)

They were later joined by the Hungarian Assault Artillery divisions. However, all this was not nearly enough to stop a possible Soviet assault.

Friessner was aware of Malinovsky's impending attack. Only weak Axis forces were available for the defence: the Hungarian 10th Infantry Division, the Hungarian 23rd Reserve Division, the Hungarian 1st Cavalry Division, the Hungarian

1st Armoured Division, the Hungarian 8th Replacement Division, the Hungarian 20th Infantry Division and the German 133rd AA Artillery Regiment.

Friessner's plan to counter the Soviet assault was to attack the undefended flanks of the attacking Soviet tank wedges with his mobile panzer formations regrouped from the Great Plain when the Soviets penetrated deep behind the defensive positions. He would then retreat and strike the Soviet flanks in other areas. In preparation, Friessner started to withdraw and regroup his panzer forces behind the front line. The 24th Panzer Division was closest, and was ordered to regroup around Kecskemét, followed by the 23rd Panzer Division, then the 18th Panzer Division, Panzer-Grenadier Division Feldherrnhalle and the German 228th Assault Artillery Brigade. As for the defence of Budapest, holding the Attila Line was vitally important: in the event of a breakthrough, the Germans would have fought to gain time, before abandoning the line and crossing over to the Buda bank and holding the line along the Danube thereafter.

SOVIET AND ROMANIAN

The Soviet attack on Budapest was to be launched on 29 October by the Soviet 46th Army in the general direction of Kecskemét and Budapest. The main assault was to be carried out by the corps forming the right wing of the army: the Soviet 10th Guards Rifle Corps, the 37th Rifle Corps and the 2nd Guards Mechanized Corps. As per the plans, the attacking Soviet forces would reach the Alberti–Örkény line by 30 October. The Soviet 31st Guards Rifle Corps on the left wing would push forwards along the Danube, with no specific target assigned. In addition, the 7th Guards Army, together with the Romanian VII Army Corps, would attack Budapest on 30 October, reaching and securing the Nagykőrös–Tószege line. The basic idea behind the plan was that the Soviet Guards Mechanized corps would quickly break through the weak, mostly Hungarian, forces and advance in depth, followed by the slower Rifle divisions. After breaking through, the Mechanized corps would move quickly on the Hungarian capital, and secure territory behind the German lines until the infantry arrived. Surprise and speed were key elements of the plan.

Once the Soviet infantry had opened a way through the Hungarian defences, the 2nd Guards Mechanized Corps would be deployed as a follow-on force. The Soviet 4th Guards Mechanized Corps and the 23rd Rifle Corps formed the reserve.

However, the road network between the Danube and the Tisza rivers was patchy, and the villages and towns along the way would no doubt become centres of resistance, slowing the advance. The aim was for the Soviet units to advance 80km in the first 36 hours, and the infantry would have to take three cities on the first day – Kecskemét, Nagykőrös and Lajosmizse. The plan's implementation was hindered by the fact that the road network between the Danube and the Tisza was patchy, and the settlements would probably become centres of resistance, slowing the advance.

Thus, the objectives were ambitious, and, moreover, the subsequent steps to take Budapest were not specified in detail. In addition, the plan did not take German reinforcements into account, trusting that they would not arrive until fighting began. All this, however, was only the opening act of the operations to take Budapest.

THE SIEGE OF BUDAPEST

THE FIRST SOVIET ATTACK: 29 OCTOBER–6 NOVEMBER 1944

Malinovsky's offensive started on 29 October between the villages of Rém and Alpár, on a 95km-wide front. Following a preparatory artillery bombardment of 30 minutes, Soviet forces attacked and broke through.

The offensive managed to break through the Hungarian positions all along the line, and inflicted heavy losses on the defenders, yet the goals set for the day were not fully achieved. Despite the breakthrough, Hungarian forces fought back hard in many places. The Hungarian 1st Armoured Division attempted to impede the main attack, which followed the Kiskunfélegyháza–Kecskemét line, but to little effect. The Hungarian units then withdrew and established a new line of defence south of Kecskemét.

Army Group South commander Friessner initially ignored the Soviet attack – he did not trust the Hungarians, and also doubted the reports he received. He expected the attack on Budapest to come from the direction of Szolnok. The German 24th Panzer Division, on the other hand, was on the move near Kecskemét that night, and ran into the Soviet forces; a struggle for the possession of Kecskemét began.

On 30 October, the vanguard of the 4th Guards Mechanized Brigade reached Kecskemét, where the units of the Hungarian 1st Cavalry Division and the Hungarian 8th Replacement Infantry Division were encamped on the outskirts of the city, and the German 23rd Panzer Division was also nearing the town's western perimeter.

The Soviets decided to try to take Kecskemét using speed. The vanguard of the 4th Guards Mechanized Brigade spearheaded the attack the following morning, but failed. Only a few T-34s managed to break through the line of defence and enter the city, but the defenders took out four Soviet tanks in short order. In parallel, further to the east, the assault of the 6th Guards Mechanized Brigade also failed, losing six tanks in the attack. After these unsuccessful efforts, the Soviets decided to encircle Kecskemét. The 4th Guards Mechanized Brigade sought to outflank the town from the west, while the 6th Guards Mechanized Brigade tried to engage the defenders from the front.

By this time, Friessner realized the aim of the Soviet attack was to take Budapest. To slow the Soviet advance, the German 4th Air Fleet increased its attacks in the area, destroying five tanks near Kecskemét that day. The

The first Soviet attack, 29 October–6 November 1944

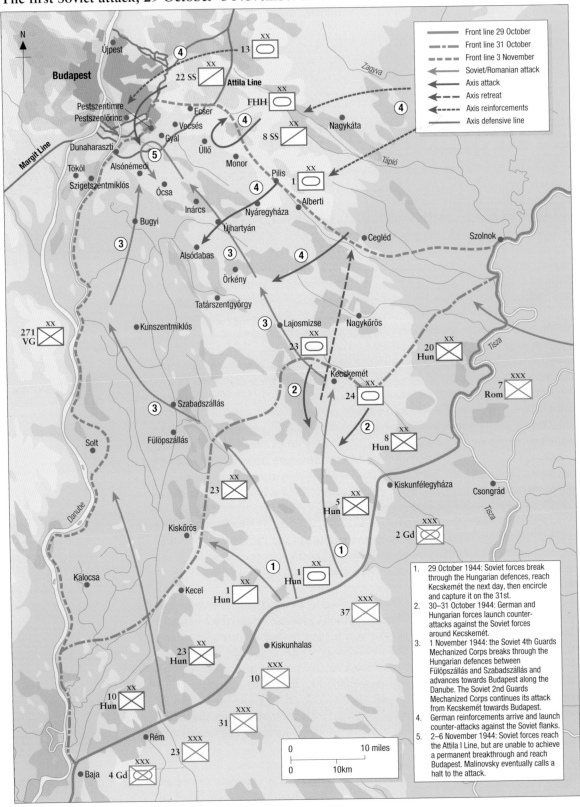

N

Budapest

Újpest

Pestszentimre
Pestszenlőrinc

Margit Line

Dunaharaszti

Tököl

Szigetszentmiklós

Ócsa

Bugyi

Alsónémedi

Gyál

Ecser

Vecsés

Üllő

Monor

Inárcs

Nyáregyháza

Újhartyán

Alsódabas

Örkény

Tatárszentgyörgy

Kunszentmiklós

Szabadszállás

Fülöpszállás

Solt

Kiskőrös

Kalocsa

Kecel

Kiskunhalas

Rém

Baja

22 SS

Attila Line

FHH

8 SS

Nagykáta

Pilis

Alberti

Cegléd

Szolnok

Lajosmizse

Nagykőrös

Kecskemét

Kiskunfélegyháza

Csongrád

13

1

23

24

20 Hun

7 Rom

8 Hun

5 Hun

2 Gd

1 Hun

37

23

10

31

23

10 Hun

23 Hun

4 Gd

271 VG

Zagyva

Tápió

Tisza

Danube

Legend:
- Front line 29 October
- Front line 31 October
- Front line 3 November
- Soviet/Romanian attack
- Axis attack
- Axis retreat
- Axis reinforcements
- Axis defensive line

1. 29 October 1944: Soviet forces break through the Hungarian defences, reach Kecskemét the next day, then encircle and capture it on the 31st.
2. 30–31 October 1944: German and Hungarian forces launch counter-attacks against the Soviet forces around Kecskemét.
3. 1 November 1944: the Soviet 4th Guards Mechanized Corps breaks through the Hungarian defences between Fülöpszállás and Szabadszállás and advances towards Budapest along the Danube. The Soviet 2nd Guards Mechanized Corps continues its attack from Kecskemét towards Budapest.
4. German reinforcements arrive and launch counter-attacks against the Soviet flanks.
5. 2–6 November 1944: Soviet forces reach the Attila I Line, but are unable to achieve a permanent breakthrough and reach Budapest. Malinovsky eventually calls a halt to the attack.

0   10 miles

0   10km

German counter-attack was to be delivered by the Hungarian 1st Armoured Division, now subordinated to the LVII Panzer Corps, and the German 1st, 23rd and 24th Panzer divisions and the German 503rd Heavy Panzer Battalion. The Hungarian counter-attack began in the morning, but soon collapsed against the Soviet defences. The German 24th Panzer Division launched an assault south of Kecskemét. Though the Soviets managed to repel the initial attack, at 1400hrs the Germans finally broke through their lines. The Germans focused their attack on one of the Soviet artillery divisions, whose 122mm howitzers used direct fire at the attacking tanks. The artillery division finally succeeded in repelling the attackers. The Soviets ordered a tank battalion to the area as reinforcement, and this helped stabilize the situation and secure the Kecskemét–Kiskunfélegyháza road.

A Soviet 152mm howitzer and its crew in Budapest. It was often used in the direct fire role from the front line to overcome resistance strongpoints. (Fortepan, 175361)

Meanwhile, the ongoing Soviet attack lacked sufficient pace to encircle Kecskemét. The 4th Guards Mechanized Brigade could not get through the Hungarian defences. The assault by one of the tank regiments of the 6th Soviet Mechanized Brigade was interrupted by a counter-attack from the 24th German Panzer Division that neutralized the Soviet assault. As reinforcements for the taking of Kecskemét, the Soviet 59th and 320th Guards Rifle divisions were also deployed, and though they managed to break in, they were only able to occupy parts of the town. The German 133rd AA Artillery Regiment and the Hungarian troops still in the town stood their ground. The Soviets lost 21 tanks over the course of the day. In contrast, the Soviets reported to have destroyed 25 tanks and assault guns, and captured 1,300 prisoners of war. Yet, they failed to reach their target for the day, the Alberti–Örkény line, mainly due to the heavy resistance around Kecskemét. The Soviet offensive against Budapest lost the element of surprise, and its momentum was also broken.

On 31 October, the Soviets managed to encircle Kecskemét, and the German 133rd AA Artillery Regiment and the other troops in the town. At the same time, the Soviets also continued their attack towards Budapest along the Kecsemét–Budapest road. German reinforcements arrived in the form of the German 1st Panzer Division, gathering near Lajosmizse. The Soviet formations were again attacked from two directions, by the Hungarian 1st Armoured Division from the west, and by the German 23rd Panzer Division from the south towards Kecskemét. Again, the Hungarian attack had little effect, but the Germans were successful, and an armoured battle soon developed. The Germans also cut off supply lines to the attacking Soviet units. The battle raged late into the night. Meanwhile, at Lajosmizse, the panzer-grenadiers of 1st Panzer Division destroyed five Soviet tanks, and succeeded in halting the Soviet 5th Guards Mechanized Brigade. By evening, the Soviets finally managed to take Kecskemét, yet the town's stalwart defenders had allowed the Germans time to regroup their reserves in Budapest.

In the wake of the Soviet late-October successes, Malinovsky reworked the attack plan. The 2nd Guards Mechanized Corps was now ordered to take Üllő and Inárcs by 2 November, then push on and take all of Budapest by 3 November. Simultaneously, the 4th Guards Mechanized Corps was ordered to reach the area of Szigetszentmiklós and Tököl by November, then break into Budapest the next day, before driving on to Újpest. The Soviet plan did not take into account German reinforcements arriving to defend Budapest – the 1st, 13th and 23rd Panzer divisions, the 22nd SS-Volunteer Cavalry Division and Panzer-Grenadier Division Feldherrnhalle – which altered the balance of the forces considerably.

On 1 November, Friessner ordered another counter-attack to halt the Soviet offensive. The German 133rd AA Artillery Regiment, which had broken out of Kecskemét, tried to establish a no-pass zone in the Lajosmizse area. The German 24th Panzer Division found itself in a tricky situation, being temporarily isolated. Meanwhile, the Soviet 2nd Guards Mechanized Corps, attempting to move towards Budapest, was halted at Lajosmizse. The German–Hungarian defensive positions established in front of the town were weak, and the defenders tried to repel the waves of Soviet attacks with armour-supported counter-attacks, but they suffered heavy losses. Friessner reorganized his troops, and the gap in the Hungarian defence was plugged by the arriving German 8th and 22nd SS-Cavalry divisions, 1st and 13th Panzer divisions, and Panzer-Grenadier Division Feldherrnhalle. However, the Soviets also received reinforcements, with the Soviet 4th Guards Mechanized Corps regrouped from Szolnok and joining the battles between Fülöpszállás and Szabadszállás on this day. The Soviets broke through the Hungarian defences, and then continued on towards Budapest along the Danube.

The Soviets launched their attack on Nagykőrös on 2 November, and managed to enter Lajosmizse in the morning. Kunszentmiklós and Tatárszentgyörgy also fell. The Soviet 2nd Guards Mechanized Corps continued to move towards Budapest. The German 1st and 23rd Panzer divisions again attacked the Soviet formations from two directions this day. The former achieved little, but the 23rd Panzer Division, attacking from the direction of Cegléd, managed to take out seven Soviet tanks, 13 AT guns and 18 trucks, for the loss of four assault guns and a Tiger. The attack was eventually called to a halt, but during the retreat, a PzKpfw V Panther and a Tiger B were blown up after becoming bogged down in mud and unable to be pulled out. The Soviet 2nd Guards Mechanized Corps lost 50 dead and 142 wounded this day, as well as 12 tanks, while destroying ten tanks, 19 SP guns and armoured vehicles and taking 180 prisoners. The Germans evacuated Lajosmizse and took up a new defensive position in Örkény, which lay on the road to Budapest and thus was important to control. The Soviet offensive had already reached Újhartyán, but due to German attacks on its flank, further Soviet progress towards Budapest was temporarily halted; instead they tried to eliminate the Germans by attacking west. By the evening, the Soviets managed to isolate Örkény, yet failed to reach their target of the Monor–Üllő–Inárcs line.

Soviet BM-13 (Katyusha) multiple rocket launchers bombarding Budapest. (TASS via Getty Images)

German counter-attacks and the defences of the settlements along the main road continued to slow the Soviet advance, and gave time for further regrouping. In the meantime, the Germans began to take up positions on the Attila Line. The chance to quickly take Budapest had evaporated.

Meanwhile, the Soviet 4th Guards Mechanized Division's attack progressed well, taking Bugyi, Ócsa and Alsónémedi, and reaching the Attila I Line, where Hungarian paratroopers were positioned. The Hungarians destroyed a tank and repulsed the Soviet attack. Though the Soviet corps had advanced 110km in one day, it was in vain, as they ran out of steam by the time of the attack on the Attila Line.

The southern part of the Attila Line was divided into two sections. The first was Defence Zone A where the German 22nd SS-Volunteer Cavalry Division and the 1st Battalion, Hungarian 1st Paratrooper Regiment, as well as three German emergency battalions were positioned. The other section was Defence Zone B, with five Hungarian Assault Artillery divisions and a German emergency battalion in the defence. In addition, the German Panzer-Grenadier Division Feldherrnhalle, 13th Panzer Division, 8th SS-Cavalry Division and the Hungarian 12th Reserve Division were also arriving, for a total force of more than 100,000 troops. On 3 November, the Soviet 2nd Guards Mechanized Corps continued its offensive along the Budapest–Cegléd route. They managed to take Üllő, taking 100 prisoners and seizing a railway train. The Germans were unaware of this, and the German 503rd Heavy Panzer Battalion, retreating to the town, thus ran into the Soviets. They lost one Tiger B tank before pulling back. The Soviet forces invading Ecser, on the other hand, were repelled by the local Hungarian troops and the Hungarian assault artillery they called in. The Soviets stopped their attack here and set for defence in Üllő. The incoming German 8th SS-Cavalry Division and Panzer-Grenadier Division Feldherrnhalle launched several unsuccessful attacks throughout the day to recapture Üllő. The Soviet 4th Guards Mechanized Brigade reached and crossed the Attila Line near Gyál on the 3rd, and occupied Vecsés, defended by only a weak Hungarian force. They continued the attack towards Ferihegy Airport, where they were hit by fire from a battery of the Hungarian 1st Assault Artillery Division, and a counter-attack pushed them back to the perimeter of Vecsés. Meanwhile, the Soviets had evacuated Vecsés, and the incoming German Panzer Division Feldherrnhalle took it without a fight. They managed to push the Soviets back behind the Attila Line in all locations. The Soviet units advancing from Gyál continued towards Pestszentimre, reaching its confines. Soviet tanks even managed to enter the town in the afternoon, but two T-34 tanks were disabled by panzerfausts.

The incursion into Pestszentimre by the Soviet 2nd Guards Mechanized Brigade should have been countered by the German 13th Panzer Division and the rest of the German and Hungarian forces that had been assigned there, but this counter-attack made further attacks on their part impossible. At this stage, they had 108 T-34s and 12 IS-2 tanks.

On 3 November, the Soviet 4th Guards Mechanized Corps renewed its attacks near Alsónémedi. The Soviet forces managed to break through the obstacles and AT ditch of the Attila I Line, but a counter-attack by the German 22nd SS-Volunteer Cavalry Division pushed the Soviets back to the ditch by evening. The German 23rd Panzer Division tried attacking the

Soviets between Alberti and Örkény to the Soviet lines of communication, but to no avail.

By the date set for taking the city, 3 November, the Soviets had not even reached Budapest. Though the Soviet 2nd and 4th Guards Mechanized corps reached the outskirts of the Hungarian capital, it was in vain as the infantry were lagging behind, and bad weather caused the Soviet air forces to suspend operations. Also, the earlier rapid advances had left some German–Hungarian resistance hotspots behind, and these further slowed both the movement of supplies and the infantry trying to catch up. The Germans ordered these remaining pockets of resistance to pull back to prevent them being wiped out. German units had suffered heavy losses in the battles so far, with 1st Panzer Division left with three PzKpfw IVs and two assault guns, and 23rd Panzer Division left with one PzKpfw IV and three PzKpfw V Panthers, four assault guns and 16 panzerjägers in serviceable condition.

Malinovsky continued to push for the seizure of Budapest. In the evening, the Soviet 23rd Rifle Corps arrived, giving him an infantry force. On 4 November, Cegléd fell, with 90 prisoners taken. However, they failed to take Alberti.

On 4 November, at dawn, the Germans launched a renewed counter-attack on Üllő at the Attila Line. Though the Soviets managed to repel this first attack, with their next attempt the Germans reached the town centre. In the end, the Soviets could only oust the Germans in house-to-house fighting.

The Soviets launched an attack on Vecsés that morning, but this was repelled by the Germans, with the assistance of Hungarian Assault Artillery units. The Soviet assault in the afternoon, however, succeeded in taking part of Vecsés.

The Soviet 4th Guards Mechanized Brigade renewed its attack on Gyál in the morning, but to no avail. They also attacked Pestszentlőrinc with the support of 30 tanks and reached its southern perimeter. But a counter-attack by the German 13th Panzer Division and Hungarian Assault Artillery units halted the Soviet attack and destroyed 20 tanks. The Germans then tried to cut off the Soviet forces that had invaded Pestszentlőrinc by means of this counter-attack and by retaking the Attila Line, but this failed.

The Soviet 2nd Guards Mechanized Corps, joined by the arriving Soviet 23rd Rifle Corps, resumed its efforts to take the Hungarian capital. They managed to occupy Alsónémedi, with the defenders retreating towards Dunaharaszti and Szigetszentmiklós. The battle for Gyál continued, and the Soviets managed to take it this day.

Friessner, on his part, planned a counter-attack by assaulting from the Szolnok–Cegléd direction, aiming to cut off the supply lines of Soviet troops nearing the southern parts of Budapest. For this attack, he waited for the German 1st Panzer Division, and he also received reinforcements from the German 23rd Panzer Division and Panzer-Grenadier Division Feldherrnhalle. The attack started on 5 November from Pilis towards the west-south-west. The Germans occupied Nyáregyháza and Újhartyán, then attacked the Soviet reinforcements along the route near Alsódabas in the evening. In this battle, they destroyed and seized a total of

Anti-tank obstacles in what is today known as Március 15 Square, near Erzsébet Bridge, Budapest. These obstacles protected the Axis bridgeheads in Pest against surprise Soviet armoured attacks. (MTI Photo Archives, 753795)

61 vehicles, 60 trucks and a T-34. Friessner discontinued the attack and regrouped his troops around Monor.

On 6 November, Malinovsky ordered the Soviet 2nd and 4th Guards Mechanized corps, and other units, to end the German incursions. With this, he withdrew these units from further attacks on Budapest. Yet, the arriving Soviet forces searched for the Germans in vain, as they were nowhere near, having retreated the day before, after their successful attack. This same day, the German 13th Panzer Division launched an attack from Monor in the direction of Vecsés, but it was not a roaring success. Malinovsky's initial attack on Budapest had lost its momentum, and the defences of the Attila Line remained intact. He had failed to win the first round of the fight for the Hungarian capital.

BUDAPEST SURROUNDED: 11 NOVEMBER –24 DECEMBER 1944

Having successfully repelled the first Soviet attack, Friessner now faced a dilemma. He could prepare to continue the fight for Budapest; there could be no doubt that the Red Army's aim was to take the Hungarian capital. Yet, the need to defend Budapest was far from self-evident. From the German point of view, the industrial capacities of the Hungarian capital were negligible, though a significant part of the country's industry was concentrated there, but this was small compared to that of the German military economy as a whole. Also, with the loss of the Danube–Tisza interfluve and the other areas east of the capital, the logistical significance of Budapest's bridges and railway lines also declined, and by the middle of December 1944, all roads and railway lines to the east were cut off due to the Soviet advances.

The whole length of the Attila Line was controlled by German and Hungarian forces, but it seemed inevitable that the Soviets would sooner or later break through, and in preparation for this, both staffs pondered as to whether it was worthwhile to defend Pest by engaging the Soviets in urban battles that would surely decimate troop numbers. The Hungarian politician Ferenc Szálasi, who became the country's leader following the attempted October switch, thought it unnecessary at this time, and called for the evacuation of the Pest bank. In November, the Hungarian leadership started evacuating state institutions and offices from the capital to the western part of the country. Friessner was also of the opinion that in the event of a breach in the Attila Line, Pest should be evacuated and any troops regrouped to the other side of the Danube. This opinion was in part grounded in the soldiers' fear, retrospectively unfounded, that Pest would witness population riots, either by the working class or the Jews in the ghetto, following the example of the 1944 Warsaw Uprising.

It was not the military leadership, nor Hungarian politicians, but Hitler who insisted on defending Budapest. He issued an order as early as 23 November that the Hungarian capital must be defended block by block, and on 1 December he followed this by declaring Budapest a Fortress City (*Festung*) in Order No. 11. This effectively meant that he forbade the troops in Budapest from abandoning the city without fighting, and should the capital be surrounded, they would have to fight to the last round. Yet, Friessner did not have sufficient reserves in November to settle in for the long-term defence of the Attila Line.

The encirclement of Budapest, 28 November–26 December 1944

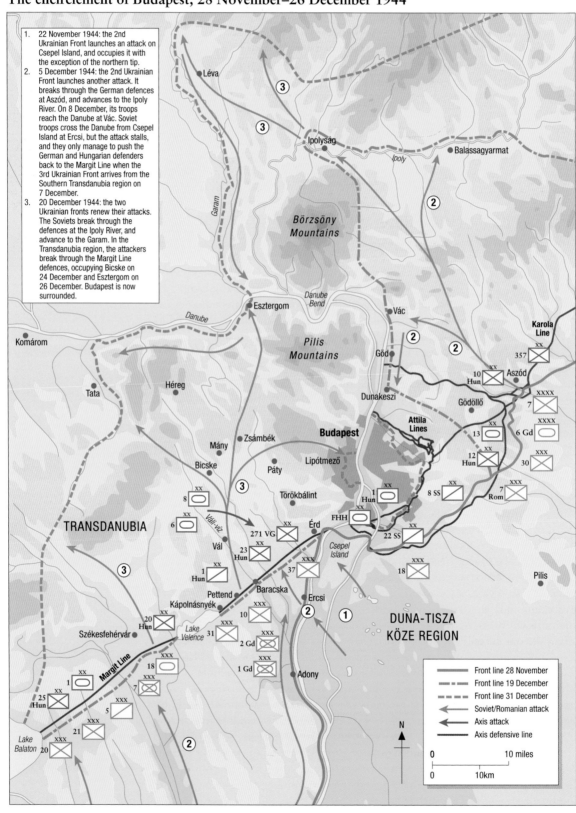

1. 22 November 1944: the 2nd Ukrainian Front launches an attack on Csepel Island, and occupies it with the exception of the northern tip.
2. 5 December 1944: the 2nd Ukrainian Front launches another attack. It breaks through the German defences at Aszód, and advances to the Ipoly River. On 8 December, its troops reach the Danube at Vác. Soviet troops cross the Danube from Csepel Island at Ercsi, but the attack stalls, and they only manage to push the German and Hungarian defenders back to the Margit Line when the 3rd Ukrainian Front arrives from the Southern Transdanubia region on 7 December.
3. 20 December 1944: the two Ukrainian fronts renew their attacks. The Soviets break through the defences at the Ipoly River, and advance to the Garam. In the Transdanubia region, the attackers break through the Margit Line defences, occupying Bicske on 24 December and Esztergom on 26 December. Budapest is now surrounded.

Léva

③

③

Ipolyság

Balassagyarmat

Ipoly

②

*Börzsöny
Mountains*

Garam

*Danube
Bend*

Esztergom

Vác

**Karola
Line**

②

XX
357

Komárom

*Pilis
Mountains*

Göd

②

XX
10
Hun

Aszód

Danube

Dunakeszi

Gödöllő

XXXX
7

Héreg

**Attila
Lines**

XX
13

XXXX
6 Gd

Tata

Zsámbék

Budapest

Lipótmező

XX
12
Hun

XXX
30

Mány

③

Bicske

Páty

Törökbálint

XX
1
Hun

XX
8 SS

XXX
7
Rom

TRANSDANUBIA

XX
8

XX
271 VG

Érd

XX
FHH

XX
6

Váli-víz

XX
23
Hun

XX
22 SS

*Csepel
Island*

XXX
18

Pilis

Vál

XXX
37

XX
1
Hun

Pettend

Baracska

Ercsi

②

①

**DUNA-TISZA
KÖZE REGION**

Kápolnásnyék

XXX
10

XX
20
Hun

*Lake
Velence*

XXX
31

Székesfehérvár

XXX
2 Gd

XXX
18

XXX
1 Gd

Adony

Margit Line

XX
1

XXX
7

XX
25
Hun

XXX
5

XX
21

*Lake
Balaton*

XXX
20

②

N

	Front line 28 November
	Front line 19 December
	Front line 31 December
	Soviet/Romanian attack
	Axis attack
	Axis defensive line

0   10 miles

0   10km

Following the failure of the first Soviet attack, Malinovsky re-evaluated the possibilities of occupying Budapest. His next objective set was to close in on Budapest from the east with the aim of encircling the Pest bridgehead. The assault that would achieve this was originally set to start on 7 November, but the German counter-offensive near the town of Pilis, launched on the 5th, delayed the Soviet attack. The Romanian VII Army Corps also formed part of the Soviet plans. The offensive was set to start from the Cegléd–Szolnok area on 7 November, but it began only on 11 November. The Soviet Pliyev Group and the

A Soviet firing position on the Buda side of the city, in a still from the Soviet movie *The Siege of Budapest*. (MTI Photo Archives, FMAFI1945_28030)

2nd and 4th Guards Mechanized corps were assigned to execute the plan, attacking from three directions simultaneously. The Germans were already preparing for an expected Soviet attack, and therefore regrouped their armoured reserves in the area, and the German 4th Air Fleet also concentrated its Hungarian forces here. The onset of the Soviet attack thus came as no surprise to the Germans, and the Soviets did not manage to breach the front line anywhere. Wet ground caused additional difficulties to the attackers, and the settlements along the roads again became hubs of resistance, costing time to overcome that the defenders used to rebuild the defences further to the rear. Friessner's troops thus were able to retreat in an orderly manner to the previously established Karola Line by 15 November.

Malinovsky now changed his previous plans to crossing over into the Transdanubia region with his forces. The first step was to occupy Csepel Island, then cross the Danube at Ercs, and from there, attack to the north and reach the Danube again at Esztergom, thus encircling Budapest from the west. But for a complete encirclement, the Soviets also had to occupy the Börzsöny Mountains on the other bank of the Danube.

The crossing to Csepel Island started on 22 November, and the Soviets occupied the whole island, with the exception of the northmost point, by 25 November; yet they were unable to cross the river. They did manage to occupy Hatvan by the 25th, but this witnessed the end of the latest Soviet–Romanian operation, and it was halted the next day. Malinovsky thus failed to achieve any breakthrough results once again, as though new territory had been gained, the taking of Budapest was not in sight. Once more, Friessner took good advantage of the terrain and the defensive lines.

In the course of the attacks on Budapest, 2nd Ukrainian Front's numbers had sharply declined, and in the second half of November, Malinovsky received an additional 40,000 troops and 200 tanks to replenish his units; also, the 30th Rifle Corps and the 18th Guards Rifle Corps were withdrawn from the 4th Ukrainian Front and placed under Malinovsky's command as further reinforcements for the attacks on Budapest. These two units would later play a key role in the fighting within the city.

On 25 November, Malinovsky formed another plan to take Budapest. The gist of it was that on 5 December, Soviet forces would attack in the north towards Ipoly, reaching the Danube, and in the south, from Csepel Island, would cross the Danube at Ercsi, and reach Esztergom, thus encircling

Budapest. They would also occupy the Buda bank of the city, thus surrounding the German and Hungarian troops stationed in the Pest bridgehead.

This time, the Soviets were successful in their endeavours. The Germans no longer had reserves in the area targeted between Aszód and Héreg, and the Soviets thus breached their defences, and then their armoured and mechanized troops pushed in to widen the breach. Following the breach, the Soviet forces had to continue the attack in three directions: towards the Danube Bend, the town of Ipolyság, and the town of Balassagyarmat.

The Soviet vanguard reached the Danube at Vác on 8 December, successfully surrounding Pest from the north. Encouraged by this, the Soviets probed Pest to see if they could capture the city, but the attack failed. To the south, they attacked towards Dunakeszi, where Panzer Division Feldherrnhalle (renamed on 27 November) was in the defence. The Soviets reached Göd on 10 December, and the next day they also managed to cross the AT ditch of the Attila I Line, and reached the Attila II positions. Malinovsky, however, halted the attack here because he had lost a total of 731 troops and 55 tanks from these units between 5 and 11 December. With this, the threat of the Soviets breaking into Pest was removed temporarily.

On the other attack wing, the 2nd Guards Mechanized Corps was set to cross the Danube from Csepel Island at Ercsi. Across the Danube, they faced the German 271st Volks-Grenadier Division (sent to the area in November), the Hungarian 1st Cavalry Division, the German 8th SS-Police Regiment and the German 239th Assault Artillery Brigade. The German 8th Panzer Division was also arriving to the area at this time. On the banks of the Danube, a system of trenches, machine-gun emplacements and earth and wood entrenchments composed the defences.

The Soviets began the crossing of the river at 2300hrs on 4 December, with 2,600 troops transported on boats. By morning, they managed to establish bridgeheads at Ercsi, but they suffered significant losses in the crossing. The next day, they captured Ercsi and on 7 December, they also took Adony. Here they joined the Transdanubia units of the 3rd Ukrainian Front attacking northwards. On 8 December, the German 8th Panzer Division launched a counter-attack against the Transdanubia Soviet units. Though the German attack slowed the Soviets, they reached the Margit Line east of Érd on 9 December, which cut the road between Lake Balaton and Budapest. They were unable to breach the line, though. The Soviets thus again failed to completely surround Budapest, and Malinovsky once again halted the operations.

Based on the partial results of the previous attack, Malinovsky reworked the earlier plan. In the north, Soviet forces were to advance to Ipoly so that the defenders in Pest could no longer be relieved from the north, and the Margit Line would be breached before reaching Esztergom, thus encircling Budapest. The attack was set to start on 20 December. Malinovsky set 23 December as the new target date for occupying the whole of Pest, and for reaching the Komárom–Nagysurány–Érsekújvár line in western Hungary by 26 December. The goals were once again over-ambitious.

Soviet A-20 Boston light bombers drop their bomb loads over Budapest. (MTI Photo Archives, 752680)

The attack along the Ipoly River, starting on 20 December, managed to break through German–Hungarian defences, and advanced towards Léva. By 28 December the Soviets fully occupied the area between the Ipoly and Hron rivers. But the task of executing the Transdanubian offensive fell to the 3rd Ukrainian Front, led by Tolbukhin, and not Malinovsky, as all Soviet forces in the Transdanubia region were assigned under the former's command. Tolbukhin's plan was to reach the Danube at Esztergom, then occupy all of Buda within five days.

Soviet riflemen riding in desant on T-34 tanks near Budapest in December 1944. (Sovfoto/ Universal Images Group via Getty Images)

At the Pest bridgehead, the Soviet 30th Rifle Corps attempted to attack in the north after 20 December, but achieved little until 25 December. The attack by the Romanian VII Army Corps was also futile, and it was discontinued on 22 December. In southern Pest, the 18th Guards Rifle Corps engaged only in minor actions between 20 and 25 December, and the situation at the Pest bridgehead thus did not change.

The Soviet attack that unfolded on 20 December achieved greatest success in the Transdanubia region. The Soviets managed to cross the Margit Line east of Lake Velence, and took Baracska, Kápolnásnyék and Pettend by evening. The Germans deployed the 6th and 8th Panzer divisions to eliminate the attackers. The Soviets, on the other hand, also deployed the 'Success Development Phase' units in the battle, but they could not drive deep behind the German defences, on account of the panzer divisions deployed by the Germans. Their armour could only advance gradually, along with the infantry. Nevertheless, by the end of the day, they had made a breach 12km wide and 8–10km deep behind the Margit Line.

On 22 December, the Soviets captured Vál and crushed the German forces there, and they also succeeded in taking Martonvásár and Tordas, thus breaking the Margit Line, which was a serious blow for the Germans and for the defence of Hungary as a whole. Colonel-General Friessner was dismissed and replaced by General Otto Wöhler. At that time, there were no significant German or Hungarian forces between the Margit Line and Esztergom. The encirclement of Budapest was only a matter of time, and the German leadership recognized this, but was no longer in a position to prevent it by this point.

On 23 December, Székesfehérvár and Zsámbék fell, and the Soviets crossed the Váli Creek. On 24 December, they took Bicske, an important railway junction on the westbound lines from Budapest, and also Perbál, Mány, Páty, and Budakeszi near Buda. The Soviet vanguard units entered Buda and reached Lipótmező, and to the south, reached the towns of Érd and Törökbálint. On 25 December, the roads running west from Budapest were all cut by the Soviets, and on 26 December, Esztergom also fell. The capital was now fully surrounded. Though once again the Soviets did not achieve their original goal of taking Budapest, the city was cut off. Now the Soviets could begin the siege of the Hungarian capital, but the Germans did not remain idle either.

TAKING PEST: 24 DECEMBER 1944
–18 JANUARY 1945

The Soviet plan was for the 37th Rifle Corps and the 2nd Guards Mechanized Corps to eliminate the Buda bridgehead within a couple of days. They would reach the Danube from the direction of Budakeszi, and split the Buda bridgehead in two before eliminating each part. All this looked good on paper, but in practice, it proved to be much more difficult.

On 24 December, the 2nd Guards Mechanized Corps occupied Budakeszi, and its recon entered Buda from the west. On the flanks, Nagy-Hárs Hill was taken, and the Hungarian AA artillery division battery there overrun without resistance, and the forward elements also reached Széchenyi Hill (its current name) before retreating after a brief firefight. The planned main direction of the attack followed the roads leading to Buda. At the Hűvösvölgyi–Nagykovácsi crossroads, the Soviets surprised a Hungarist battle group, and had them surrounded in a villa. These, however, were just preparatory Soviet moves to assess the resistance to be expected in Buda.

In southern Buda, the 2nd Guards Mechanized Corps also tried to take Budaörs but the Panzer Division Feldherrnhalle armoured battle group repelled the Soviet attack.

In northern Pest, the Soviet 30th Rifle Corps unsuccessfully tried to break through between Fót and Rákospalota. The Romanian VII Army Corps was on the defensive all through the day. In southern Pest, the Soviet 18th Guards Rifle Corps renewed the attacks on the Attila I Line, and they managed to break through it in a few places, but their attacks around Maglód, Vecsés and Gyál this day failed to achieve anything. The attacks on southern Buda were supported by Il-2 assault fighters of the 17th Soviet Air Army.

On 25 December, the main force of the Soviet 2nd Guards Mechanized Corps entered Budapest along Budakeszi Road, and the Soviet 108th Guards Rifle Division occupied János Hill and Széchenyi Hill, and reached Lipótmező in the north and Zugliget in the south. The Soviets advanced all the way to the Új Szent János Hospital, though the defenders tried to slow the attack and even destroyed three IS-2 tanks. The defenders also launched two counter-attacks: the first by German AA artillery units supported by SP guns, the other by the Budapest Guards Battalion and gendarmes supported by Hungarian Zrínyi assault howitzers. They managed to eject the Soviet troops from the hospital back along Budakeszi Road to the János Hill–Nagy-Hárs Hill line, but on the flanks the Soviets maintained their positions. At this stage, there was no continuous front line between Budakeszi and Budaörs, with both the defenders and attackers moving along the main roads and the flanks as yet unsecured. Neither side had sufficient infantry units to control the area.

In Buda, the Soviet 37th Guards Tank Brigade, now reinforced by the 320th Rifle Division, launched another attack on Budaörs, losing at least five T-34s but failing to achieve results. Budaörs Airport was lost, but a Ju 52 transport and a courier plane still had time to take off before the Soviets arrived.

A force of Soviet Il-2 Sturmovik ground attack aircraft over Budapest, with the Danube, Margit Island and the Parliament visible below. Over the course of the siege of Budapest, Il-2 fighters provided most of the air support during the ground battles. (MTI Photo Archives, 752895)

The Pest bridgehead, 26 December 1944–18 January 1945

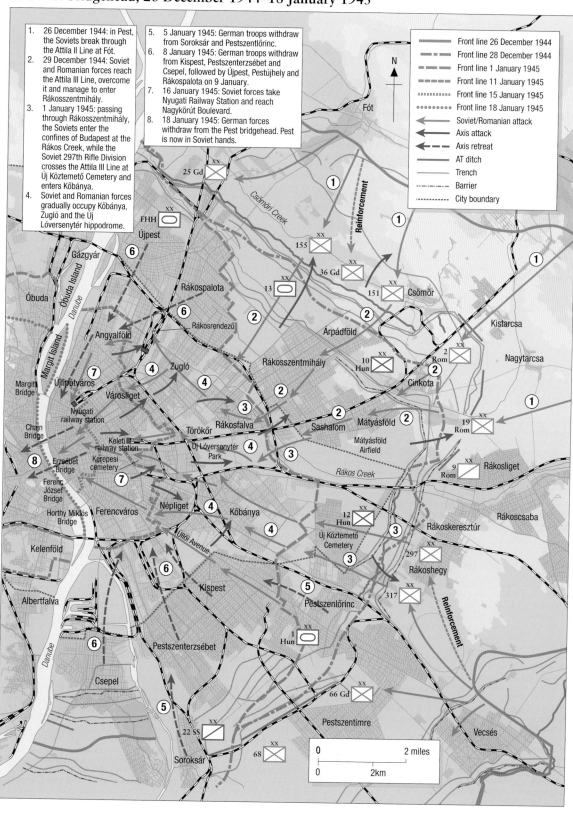

1. 26 December 1944: in Pest, the Soviets break through the Attila II Line at Fót.
2. 29 December 1944: Soviet and Romanian forces reach the Attila III Line, overcome it and manage to enter Rákosszentmihály.
3. 1 January 1945: passing through Rákosszentmihály, the Soviets enter the confines of Budapest at the Rákos Creek, while the Soviet 297th Rifle Division crosses the Attila III Line at Új Köztemető Cemetery and enters Kőbánya.
4. Soviet and Romanian forces gradually occupy Kőbánya, Zugló and the Új Lóversenytér hippodrome.

5. 5 January 1945: German troops withdraw from Soroksár and Pestszentlőrinc.
6. 8 January 1945: German troops withdraw from Kispest, Pestszenterzsébet and Csepel, followed by Újpest, Pestújhely and Rákospalota on 9 January.
7. 16 January 1945: Soviet forces take Nyugati Railway Station and reach Nagykörút Boulevard.
8. 18 January 1945: German forces withdraw from the Pest bridgehead. Pest is now in Soviet hands.

	Front line 26 December 1944
	Front line 28 December 1944
	Front line 1 January 1945
	Front line 11 January 1945
	Front line 15 January 1945
	Front line 18 January 1945
	Soviet/Romanian attack
	Axis attack
	Axis retreat
	AT ditch
	Trench
	Barrier
	City boundary

Also on 25 Decemeber, the Soviet 23rd Rifle Corps and the 99th Rifle Division took Törökbálint, the Soviet 83rd Naval Infantry Brigade took Nagytétény, and the 316th Rifle Division occupied Budatétény and then Budafok. The Hungarian AA Artillery Division was also dislodged from near Kamaraerdő and withdrew to Buda, spiking the guns it left behind.

After the redeployment of the German 8th SS-Cavalry Division, only Panzer Division Feldherrnhalle, the Hungarian 4th Cavalry Regiment and the German 13th Panzer Division remained in northern Pest, under the command of Major-General Schmidhuber. The central sector was defended by the Hungarian 10th Infantry Division, 12th Reserve Division and 1st Armoured Division, and the Assault Artillery divisions led by Ernő Billnitzer. Southern Pest, including the northern tip of Csepel Island, was defended by the German 22nd SS-Volunteer Cavalry Division under the command of *SS-Brigadeführer* August Zehender.

In northern Pest, the Soviet 30th Rifle Corps tried to break through the defences of the Attila II Line between Fót and Rákospalota but were once again unsuccessful. It had been reinforced with a tank battalion, and the redeployed 155th Rifle Division was also joining the 151st Rifle Division, leaving their front line sector to the 25th Guards Rifle Division. The Romanian VII Army Corps remained on the defensive. In southern Pest, the Soviet 18th Guards Rifle Corps renewed its attacks around Vecsés, where it successfully breached the Attila I Line. To counter this, the Hungarian 1st Armoured Division was deployed; it suffered heavy losses in the fighting and was unable to counter the incursion, but it stopped the Soviets from gaining further ground. The 18th Guards Rifle Corps lost 201 troops this day.

On 26 December, Budakalász and Békásmegyer, north of Buda, fell into Soviet hands without significant fighting. The Soviet 108th Rifle Division occupied all of Lipótmező and also reached Pasarét. In central Buda, in parallel with a German regrouping, the Soviets increased their forces, and the Soviet 59th Rifle Division arrived, joining the fighting south of the 108th Rifle Division. In southern Buda, the Soviet 316th Rifle Division occupied Budafok and Albertfalva, and broke into Kelenföld. Nine Hungarian Zrínyi assault guns and German panzer-grenadiers reassigned from Pest launched a counter-attack and breached the positions of one of the Soviet regiments. On the Soviet side, the Soviet SP artillery and riflemen deployed as reinforcements pushed the defenders back to Kelenföld Railway Station and destroyed two Zrínyi assault howitzers. The retreating German forces shelled ammunition wagons at the train station, and the explosion destroyed the surrounding buildings. The Germans tried to recapture the station with another attack, but to no avail. This day, the Germans also launched another unsuccessful counter-attack towards Budaörs Airport. The first Soviet recon troops now reached the Lágymányos Railway Embankment, already heavily fortified. This embankment was the line of defence that stood the longest during the siege, lasting six weeks. Tanks were unable to cross the embankment; the roads passing beneath the railway lines were protected with AT guns, and the bridges later were blown

Soviet riflemen in Budafok. Note the 7.62mm DT machine gun in the left foreground. (Sovfoto/Universal Images Group via Getty Images)

up, making the roads impassable. The embankment itself was laid with mines, a line of fire-trenches was established, and dense barbed wire was spread in three rows. Behind the wire barriers, machine-gun nests were established at eight strongpoints along the length of the embankment. A covered and camouflaged trench connected the embankment to the buildings behind, which were filled with troops and machine-gun nests. These houses formed the second line of defence. The flat, unprotected area north of the embankment had only a few buildings; if the Soviets broke through the embankment, they would be exposed to fire in this open area from the second-line machine guns.

Soviet riflemen move forward, supported by a T-34 tank, along a Budapest street. (MTI Photo Archives, 753063)

In northern Pest, the 155th and 151st Rifle divisions of the Soviet 30th Rifle Corps launched an attack along the Fót–Rákospalota main road. The joint attack, aided by reinforcements, managed to overcome the Hungarian defences, despite the loss of several tanks. Panzer Division Feldherrnhalle was deployed but was unable to reverse the situation. In southern Pest, the attack by the Soviet 18th Guards Rifle Corps' 68th Guards Rifle Division in Soroksár was unsuccessful against the German 22nd SS-Volunteer Cavalry Division. Near Vecsés, the Soviet 66th Guards Rifle Division continued the previous days' attack and managed to reach and cut the main Vecsés–Ecser road. German and Hungarian troops launched several counter-attacks against the Soviet incursions here, but to no avail. The Hungarian 1st Armoured Division suffered further heavy losses on this day, as did the Hungarian Billnitzer Group's Assault Artillery divisions defending against the attacks of the Soviet 317th Rifle Division from Maglód to Ecser.

The situation facing *SS-Obergruppenführer* Pfeffer-Wildenbruch was becoming all the more difficult as, besides the increasing pressure in Buda, he also had to deal with the heavy incursions at Fót. He thus tried to deploy his existing reserves at Fót, including the Hungarian Vannay Battalion regrouped from Buda.

On 27 December, in northern Buda, the Soviet 109th Guards Rifle Division occupied Csillaghegy and Rómaifürdő without major fighting, then continued to advance south, securing the strongpoint of Óbuda Railway Station. In central Buda, Soviet troops again reached the Új Szent János Hospital and occupied it. In addition, the Soviet 108th Guards Rifle Division, reinforced with additional artillery units, tried to advance further towards the Danube but due to the defences consolidating, it only partly succeeded, reaching Zöldmál in the north and Orbán Hill in the south. The Soviet 59th Rifle Division reached Orbán Hill at the same time, and also Márton Hill. In southern Buda, Soviet forces continued to slowly gain ground. The Soviet 320th Rifle Division occupied Budaörs, and even managed to temporarily take Dobogó Hill before it was recaptured by the Germans the same day. The Soviet 23rd Rifle Corps had already penetrated deep into Kelenföld, but Kelenföld Railway Station was retaken with a counter-attack.

Pfeffer-Wildenbruch abandoned Budaörs, thus shortening the front line to free up troops to counter enemy pressure in southern Buda. Also, Buda had no prepared fortifications, unlike the Attila Line in Pest. Only impromptu obstacles were set up, and the defenders also tried to take advantage of the terrain for protection.

In northern Pest, the Germans began evacuating Dunakeszi in the wake of the Fót breach and retreated to Újpest and Rákospalota. The Soviets further deepened the breach near Fót that the 30th Rifle Corps had made the previous day. Here, a successful German counter-attack destroyed four Soviet tanks and inflicted significant losses on Soviet infantry, but a group of the Hungarian 4th Hussar Regiment surrendered. The Soviet attacks, however, could not be successfully halted. The defenders reinforced Csömör, but the Soviets avoided the town. In response, the Hungarians launched a counter-attack with the Hungarian forces assigned to counter the Fót incursion, and this pushed back the Soviets from around Csömör, before collapsing. Some Soviet forces advanced to the outskirts of Árpádföld this day.

In the wake of the Soviet successes, the Romanian VII Army Corps renewed its attacks near Isaszeg, which had failed to yield results on 20 December. This time, they managed to break through the Attila II Line, forcing the Hungarian 12th Reserve Division here to retreat to the Attila III Line in the direction of Cinkota.

In southern Pest, the Soviet 18th Guards Rifle Corps continued its attack from the previous day, trying to further exploit its successes. The Soviet 68th Guards Rifle Division continued its effort to take Gyál but was unable to fully occupy it by evening. At the same time, the Soviet 66th Guards Rifle Division took Vecsés that day, breaching the Attila I Line. The 317th Rifle Division renewed its attacks at Maglód, where the Hungarian 1st Armoured Division attempted to counter-attack before running out of momentum. The Hungarian troops here retreated to the Rákoshegy–Ecser line, but later that day Rákoshegy, Ecser and Maglód fell. The Soviet attack was only halted at the Attila III Line on the outskirts of Budapest. The Hungarian 1st Armoured Division was completely broken by the day's battles, and only the Billnitzer Group remained in defence. The most stable sector of the southern Pest defences was that of the German 22nd SS-Volunteer Cavalry Division. The Soviet 18th Guards Rifle Corps lost 208 troops this day and captured only 20 prisoners.

Holding the Budapest pocket depended to a large extent on supply. On 25 December, Hitler ordered that air supplies to Budapest be organized, but it was only on the 27th that the Budapest Supply Staff at Pápa was established by the German 4th Air Fleet. The staff, under Lieutenant-General Gerhard Conrad, comprised two German transport divisions and two Hungarian transport companies, flying Ju 52s and DFS-230 cargo gliders. Supply runs were also supported by He 111 bombers taking off from Érsekújvár and Wiener Neustadt. The Germans were no longer able to secure the lasting air superiority over Budapest needed for successful air supply missions, and could only manage temporary fighter support. In liaison with Army Group South, the Budapest Supply Staff set a target of delivering 80 tons of supplies (ammunition, fuel, food and medical) per day, of which 60 tons by transports and 20 tons by airdrop. The transports, however, required airfield, and these were either lost or were soon within Soviet artillery range – Budaörs on 25 December, Ferihegy on the 27th and Mátyásföld on the 30th.

As such, establishing emergency airfields became an urgent priority, in the form of the sportsfield in northern Csepel and the Új Lóversenytér hippodrome. Andrássy Avenue was also considered as an alternative runway, but the idea was eventually discarded. For the airdrops, drop zones were designated, such as the old hippodrome, the Kisrákos training ground and Vérmező Park. The latter became more and more prominent as the siege progressed.

This German DFS 230 cargo glider crashed into the building at 35 Attila Street, on the Pest bank, on 4 February 1945. Among other supplies, the plane was transporting flour. The pilot was killed in the crash, and his flour-covered corpse was only recovered from the building in the summer of 1945. (Fortepan, 175256)

After Pfeffer-Wildenbruch withdrew the 8th SS-Cavalry Division from the Pest bridgehead, the Soviets breached the Attila II Line in the north and the Attila I Line in the south. The former Pest bridgehead defensive lines could not be held with the forces available, so Pfeffer-Wildenbruch withdrew his units to the shorter Attila III Line, stabilizing the defences.

Malinovsky felt that the elimination of the Pest bridgehead was now in sight, and even believed that after being surrounded on the Buda side, the Germans might give up the Pest bridgehead altogether. He reinforced the 30th Rifle Corps with three artillery brigades, and the 18th Guards Rifle Corps with two artillery brigades, ten T-34 tanks and the 297th Soviet Rifle Division. The strength of the 297th was significantly higher (about 6,000 troops) than that of the other Soviet divisions fighting around the Pest bridgehead (*c.* 4,000 troops each). In the operations to follow, this division spearheaded the taking of the Pest bridgehead. Soviet artillery now had to provide direct fire support to the assault teams from the front line. Malinovsky expected the newly deployed forces to split the bridgehead in two by reaching the Danube, before surrounding the defenders and eliminating them.

On 28 December, the Soviet 109th Guards Rifle Division was able to advance in Óbuda along Bécsi Road to Remete Hill and the old Óbuda Cemetery, where they were halted by the German defences established there. The Germans demolished the Northern Railway Bridge on this day.

The Soviet 180th Rifle Division was transferred to Óbuda. Tolbukhin, however, feared a possible German sortie towards Pilis, and prepared to counter this. At Remete Hill, the Hungarian Academy Assault Battalion (without orders) did indeed try to break out, but failed. A group of Academy students ended up trapped in a restaurant at the foot of Remete Hill.

Tolbukhin made further changes to his plans, as the Buda bridgehead had not been split in half and eliminated as expected. He withdrew the 2nd Guards Mechanized Corps from Buda, ceding its front line sector to the 108th Guards Rifle Division which turned over its positions on Orbán Hill to the 59th Guards Rifle Division. Yet, despite the arrival of artillery support, the 108th Guards Rifle Division was unable to make substantial progress. The 59th Soviet Rifle Division occupied the outskirts of Farkasréti Cemetery, and demolished the cemetery church tower, where a German artillery observer was stationed.

In southern Buda, the 99th Soviet Rifle Division failed to take Dobogó Hill, and were deep inside Kelenföld. The 83rd Naval Infantry Brigade reached the Lágymányos Railway Embankment. The Germans demolished the Southern Railway Bridge.

In northern Pest, the Panzer Division Feldherrnhalle pulled out of Dunakeszi and retreated to the Attila III Line. The 30th Soviet Rifle Corps continued its attack, crossing Csömöri Creek. Panzer Division Feldherrnhalle launched several counter-attacks against the Soviets, but failed to halt them. Csömör was overrun, but the Germans then recaptured it with a counter-attack.

The Romanian VII Army Corps continued to pursue the retreating Hungarians, captured Kistarcsa and Nagytarcsa, and launched an attack on Cinkota, which was countered by the Hungarian defenders on the Attila III Line. That same day, the Romanians also occupied Pécel, Rákoscsaba and Rákosliget, but their advance stalled on the Attila III Line.

In southern Pest, having been reinforced the previous day, the Soviet 18th Guards Rifle Corps renewed its attacks and took Pestszentlőrinc, Pestszentimre and Gyál. Attempting to breach the Attila III Line, the Soviet tanks managed to push into Kispest, where the Germans sent in assault guns. In the ensuing battle, the Soviets lost five tanks and the Germans two assault guns. The remaining Soviet tanks retreated, and the Hungarian and German defenders held their Attila III Line positions. The 18th Guards Rifle Corps also tried to break the line at Rákoskeresztúr, which was now defended by an infantry group of the Hungarian Assault Artillery, but this too was unsuccessful. The Soviet 18th Guards Rifle Corps captured 250 prisoners this day and received an additional artillery brigade as reinforcement. Despite the pressure, the Attila III Line held.

On 29 December, in Óbuda, the Soviet 180th Rifle Division regrouped, and was reinforced with an artillery and a mortar brigade. The newly arrived 180th Rifle Division took over the front line sector around Bécsi Road from the 109th Guards Rifle Division. Their attack, however, was unsuccessful. The 109th Guards Rifle Division's front line was shortened to extend only to the Danube, and they made significant advances here, occupying the semi-developed outskirts of the city (Rómaifürdő and the Gas Factory), and reaching the centre of Óbuda.

In central Buda, the 108th Guards Rifle Division renewed its attacks from the previous day, but were unsuccessful, and the Germans even launched three counter-attacks.

The ruins of the funeral building in Farkasréti Cemetery. (Fortepan, 72959)

In southern Buda, German and Hungarian forces launched a counter-attack from the Lágymányos Railway Embankment. The Hungarian Budapest Battalion and Hungarian Zrínyi assault howitzers took part in the attack, with a Hungarian Buzogányvető AT rocket in support. This attack was one of the greatest Axis successes during the siege, pushing the Soviet troops back c. 1.5km, but by the end of the day the front stabilized again along the Ság Hill–Farkasréti Cemetery line on the Lágymányos Railway Embankment. For the rest of the siege, these remained the corner bastions of the defence in the southern Buda sector.

In northern Pest, the Soviet 30th Rifle Corps reached the Attila III Line on the outskirts of Újpest and successfully crossed the Attila III Line at Árpádföld, the Soviet 155th Rifle Division broke into Rákosszentmihály and the 151st Rifle Division occupied Csömör.

The Romanian VII Army Corps also breached the Attila III Line, and reached the eastern perimeters of Mátyásföld, but a counter-attack by the Hungarian 12th Reserve Division pushed them back to the line.

In southern Pest, despite all the reinforcements, the Soviet 18th Guards Rifle Corps was unable to achieve results with its attack on the Attila III, as the German and Hungarian defenders held the line. The defenders also launched a number of counter-attacks that caused heavy losses to the Soviets.

On the 29th, the Soviets sent two parlimentaires bearing a surrender ultimatum to the commander-in-chief of the defending forces. Captain Ilya Afanasyevich Ostapenko, in Buda, crossed the front line at Budaörsi Road and was then escorted to the Gellért Hill positions of the 8th SS-Cavalry Division. There, he handed over the ultimatum, but was killed by Soviet mortar fire when returning. In Pest, Hungarian-born Soviet Captain Miklós Steinmetz tried to get through the German positions on Üllői Avenue, but his vehicle struck a mine, and he was killed. A firefight ensued. Soviet propaganda long blamed their deaths on the enemy, claiming they were deliberately shot by the Germans.

On 30 December, in northern Buda, the Soviet 180th Rifle Division occupied Zöldmál and established contact with the 108th Guards Rifle Division, thereby establishing a continuous front line in Buda. The 180th managed to occupy the northern parts of Remete Hill, and the old Óbuda Cemetery. The Soviet 109th Guards Rifle Division reached Schmidt Castle, a German strongpoint in Óbuda.

In central Buda, the 108th Guards Rifle Division launched another attack, but was halted at the BBTE Sports Ground and Plant Protection Research Institute building, both of which were German strongholds that held out for almost a month. Also, though the Soviets managed to occupy the Rókus Hill fortifications, as a result of German counter-attacks the hill became a no-man's-land by the end of the day. The Soviets even lost two SP guns here. In southern Buda, the defenders of the Farkasréti Cemetery repelled a Soviet attack.

In Pest, the fighting on this day focused on the centre of the bridgehead, seeking to control Rákosszentmihály. The defenders temporarily encircled a Soviet assault group there that fought surrounded all day, before breaking out. The defenders also launched a number of counter-attacks against the Soviets. The Romanian VII Army Corps occupied Cinkota, and also broke through the Hungarian 12th Reserve Division positions, occupying Mátyásföld, including the local airfield. In southern Pest, the situation remained unchanged; the attacks by the Soviet 18th Guards Rifle Corps failed, and they lost 632 troops over two days.

The 17th Soviet Air Army was deployed in 87 missions over Budapest at night, and Il-2 ground-attack aircraft targeted Budapest in 28 deployments by day. The Soviet 5th Air Army was deployed in 55 missions against Budapest at night but was not deployed against the capital by day. Two Ju 52 planes of the German Budapest Supply Staff landed successfully at the Új Lóversenytér airfield for the first time, delivering about four tons of supplies and evacuating 18 wounded troops. In addition, an unknown number of He 111 planes flew over Budapest, delivering airdrops.

The heavily damaged Schmidt Castle in Óbuda, which served as a strongpoint in the German defences. (Fortepan, 155537)

On 31 December, in Óbuda, the Soviet 180th Guards Rifle Division attempted to occupy the critical position of Schmidt Castle, but was repulsed. In the battle for Óbuda, the Soviets lost 246 troops over three days.

In southern Buda, the 99th Soviet Rifle Division occupied Dobogó Hill and the southern parts of Kelenföld Railway Station. The Soviets also launched an attack on the Lágymányos Railway Embankment but were repelled by the defenders, who replied with a counter-attack. However, the latter inflicted such losses on the Budapest Battalion that they had to be withdrawn and were replaced on the embankment by the battle group led by Major Gyula Viharos. The defences of the Buda bridgehead were now established, and settled for several weeks, with the cornerstones of defence being Schmidt Castle, Városmajor Park and the nearby fortifications, Farkasréti Cemetery, Sas Hill and the Lágymányos Railway Embankment.

In Pest, the attacks still focused on the central sector: in Rákosszentmihály, the Soviet 151st and 155th Rifle divisions fought off several counter-attacks by Panzer Division Feldherrnhalle, then eventually occupied the majority of the area and reached the outskirts of Budapest. The defenders captured Mátyásföld Airport for a time. The Soviet 18th Rifle Corps' attacks in southern Pest still failed to achieve any results.

On 1 January 1945, the Soviet 109th Guards Rifle Division attempted another attack on Schmidt Castle in Óbuda, but to no avail, and it lost 133 troops. The Soviet 180th Rifle Division, on the other hand, successfully captured Mátyás Hill.

In Városmajor Park, a Soviet attack captured part of the area, but the Hungarian Vannay Battalion recaptured it with a counter-attack the same day. The Vannay Battalion then followed by establishing a triple line of defence here. The first line was at the embankment of the Cog-wheel Railway, and included wire barriers and a minefield, covered by four machine-gun nests. The second line was at Temes Street, based on the air-raid trenches there, and covered by an AA machine cannon and machine guns emplaced in the buildings around the park. The third line was at Szamos Street, with barbed-wire barriers and gunpits with machine guns to the rear.

In southern Buda, the Soviets managed to clear Kelenföld and closed on the whole length of the Lágymányos Railway Embankment. The Soviet naval infantry attacked the embankment once more, but again to no avail. The Hungarian AT Morlin Group defending the embankment was reassigned to Pest. During the day, the Germans launched a number of armour-supported counter-attacks against the Soviets near Budaörsi Road and Kelenföld.

In central Pest, the 151st and 155th Rifle divisions invaded Rákosfalva and reached the Rákos Stream defence line. The defending Feldherrnhalle and 13th Panzer divisions launched five counter-attacks backed by tanks, yet to no avail. Sashalom, on the other hand, was captured. Rákos Creek was a further line of defence established within the city, with the creek bed sewn with mines, continuous barbed-wire barriers on the north bank, a trench system on the south bank, and nearby stone buildings converted to strongpoints.

The Romanian VII Army Corps continued its assault along Kerepesi Road and also reached Rákos Creek, capturing 300 Hungarian prisoners and the Kisrákos training grounds.

In southern Pest, the 18th Guards Rifle Corps elected to concentrate its attack on a narrow area in an effort to breach the Attila III Line at Új-Köztemető Cemetery and the drive on into the capital towards Kőbánya. The task was assigned to the Soviet 297th Rifle Division, supported by four artillery brigades, a tank company and two assault engineer battalions. The 297th had been rested and remanned, and received intensive training throughout December to prepare for urban combat. It took over the positions of the 317th Rifle Division, and set up assault groups specifically for the urban battles. The attack was preceded by a massive artillery bombardment, and in its wake, it broke through the Hungarian Attila III defences in about half an hour, capturing Új-Köztemető Cemetery and breaking into Kőbánya. The other divisions of the Soviet 18th Rifle Corps failed to make any notable gains.

Soviet and Romanian troops occupied around 200 blocks in Budapest this day. For Pfeffer-Wildenbruch, the situation in Pest again became critical with the Attila III Line broken and the Soviets having pushed into Kőbánya and Zugló. He was forced to deploy his remaining reserves. In Buda, in contrast, the defence had stabilized; but receiving adequate supplies was crucial, and thus control of Új Lóversenytér airfield was paramount.

On 2 January, in Óbuda, the Soviet 109th Guards Rifle Division attempted another unsuccessful attack on Schmidt Castle. The Germans tried to recapture Mátyás Hill, lost the day before, with tank support, but achieved only partial success. In southern Buda, the Soviet naval infantry launched another unsuccessful attack on the Lágymányos Railway Embankment, but in its eastern sector, the Soviets managed to cross the embankment and gained some ground beyond it.

In northern Pest, the Soviet 25th Guards Rifle Division reached the outskirts of Pestújhely, and the 155th and 151st Rifle divisions repelled German tank-supported attacks, crossed the Rákos Creek and broke into Zugló. German counter-attacks managed to prevent the Soviets from gaining further ground.

Hungarian prisoners of war on Kinizsi Street in Pest. On the left of the picture is a hussar. (Fortepan, 175237)

The Romanian VII Army Corps was also slow to advance, and reached only the Éles Sarok junction. Opposite, the fighting strength of the Hungarian 12th Infantry Division's battalions was now below 30 troops. The German emergency airfield at Új Lóversenytér was now within mortar range, but landings continued. The Soviet 297th Rifle Division continued to fight in eastern Kőbánya, capturing local factories. On the 2nd, they lost 161 troops and took 220 prisoners. The rest of the 18th Soviet Rifle Corps made no advances.

On 3 January, in Óbuda, the Soviet 109th Guards Rifle Division attempted

THE LÁGYMÁNYOS RAILWAY EMBANKMENT, 0800HRS, 2 JANUARY 1945 (PP. 46–47)

The Lágymányos Railway Embankment (**1**) formed a key line of the Axis defence for about six weeks during the siege of Budapest. Soviet armour could not break through this line because the railway embankment was so steep. The roads passing through the embankment were blocked by the defenders by demolishing the bridges above them (**2**). Thus, only infantry troops could overcome this obstacle. Facing the attacking Soviet and Romanian infantry were three rows of barbed-wire barriers extending along the embankment (**3**), and machine-gun emplacements were emplaced on the top of the embankment in the northern section (**4**). A second line of defence was established in the buildings behind the embankment

(**5**). Those attacking Soviet troops that crossed the embankment reached an open, flat area where they would then be pinned down by gunfire from the defenders in the surrounding buildings.

At the end of December 1944, a Hungarian *kampfgruppe* led by Major Gyula Viharos took over the defence of the embankment in the section from Fehérvári Road to the Danube. On 2 January 1945, the embankment was again attacked, but the Viharos *kampfgruppe* repelled the assault. A lull followed. In the days before the fall of the Pest bridgehead (18 January 1945), the Soviets once again attacked the embankment, but would not be able to break through until 10 February.

another unsuccessful attack on Schmidt Castle. The Germans managed to capture the whole of Máytás Hill on this day, but it changed hands seven times. The Hungarian Academy Assault Battalion also joined in the fighting here. The 108th Guards Rifle Division discontinued their attacks against Buda, and moved to the defensive. The 320th Rifle Division's assault on Sas Hill was repulsed by the defenders. The defences there were complete. The steep rocky slopes to the south formed a natural obstacle. To the west side of the hill, a wire barrier extended in front of the first defensive line, and a second line was also established behind. The western slope could only be approached with a frontal attack, and to the east, minefields were laid, and German assault guns and Hungarian assault howitzers also gave occasional support.

In Pest, the 155th Soviet Rifle Division reached Zugló, but could not cross Rákos Creek. The Soviet 151st Rifle Division pushed deep into Zugló. On the 3rd, the Soviet 30th Rifle Corps was reinforced with the 36th Guards Rifle Division, and it promptly crossed Rákos Creek. Almost all of Rákosfalva was captured that day. The Romanian VII Army Corps gradually neared Új Lóversenytér airfield, where two dug-in tanks bolstered the defence. The Soviet air forces mistakenly attacked the Romanian units on this day.

The Soviet 18th Guards Rifle Corps withdrew the 66th Guards Rifle Regiment and reassigned it to Kőbánya, escalating the military operations there. The 297th Rifle Division shortened its Kőbánya front line so that the newly arriving 66th could take it over. The 297th captured the central parts of Kőbánya and also reached Új Lóversenytér airfield. They lost 123 troops on this day, captured 74 prisoners and reported seven German tanks destroyed. Soviet troops occupied 155 blocks in Kőbánya by day's end. In southern Pest, the Soviet attacks against the German 22nd SS-Volunteer Cavalry Division still failed to achieve a breakthrough. In total, 167 blocks in Budapest were taken by Soviet and Romanian forces on the 3rd.

In Buda the following day, Soviet forces recaptured Mátyás Hill and launched an attack against Látó and Remete hills. In southern Buda, the Soviet 99th Rifle Division was withdrawn, and the rest of the Soviet forces here also suspended further attacks on account of the *Konrad* operations underway.

In Buda, the Soviet 37th Rifle Corps took over the 23rd Army Corps' front. The majority of the Soviet 59th Guards Rifle Division, the 99th Rifle Division and supporting artillery were withdrawn to counter *Konrad*, and most of the air support was also deployed against the German relief attempts. The 37th Rifle Corps moved to the defence and prepared for a possible breakout by the defenders, erecting barriers and obstacles. The positions of the withdrawn 59th Guards Rifle Division were taken over by the 108th Guards Rifle Division, extending its own front line. The 99th Rifle Division was replaced by the 316th Rifle Division, also extending its frontage. Soviet forces in Buda mostly shifted to the defence until 12 January.

In Pest, the Soviet 25th Guards Rifle Division tried to break into Pestújhely, but to no avail. In central Pest, the fight for Zugló

A Soviet scout equipped with a sub-machine gun and a bicycle at Kálvária Square in Pest. Note the German 10.5cm howitzer in the background. (Fortepan, 58303)

continued, with nine German armour-supported counter-attacks failing to stop the Soviet advance. The Romanian VII Army Corps secured Rákosfalva and the eastern half of Új Lóversenytér airfield, impeding Axis air supply. The Germans counter-attacked with some success, but after losing two tanks, the Romanians retook the eastern areas, losing 111 troops in the course of the day. The Soviet 18th Guards Rifle Corps pushed on, taking 65 city blocks on the 4th. The Soviet 297th Rifle Division continued to clear Kőbánya and attacked towards Kerepes Cemetery, taking 194 casualties overall. On their flank, however, the 66th Rifle Division captured only 15 blocks, losing 157 troops and capturing 194 prisoners. Soviet and Romanian forces captured 277 blocks in total in Budapest on this day.

On 5 January, the defenders repelled the Soviet 320th Rifle Division's attack on Farkasréti Cemetery in Buda. In parallel, the Soviets launched another attack between Farkasréti Cemetery and Sas Hill, and managed to secure further buildings.

In Pest, the fight for Zugló continued, with the Soviet 30th Rifle Corps capturing 30 blocks. The Romanian VII Army Corps broke into Törökőr. The 18th Guards Rifle Corps occupied the rest of Kőbánya and reached the edge of Népliget. The Romanians failed to force the German defenders out of Új Lóversenytér airfield. The German 22nd SS-Volunteer Cavalry Division evacuated Soroksár and Pestszentlőrinc, and took over the Kőbánya front. The Soviet 68th Guards Rifle Division occupied Soroksár and Pestszentlőrinc.

To strengthen the defences of the Pest bridgehead, Pfeffer-Wildenbruch regrouped parts of the German 271st Volks-Grenadier Division and the Panzer Division Feldherrnhalle *kampfgruppe*, plus artillery, to Pest from Buda. Soviet and Romanian forces captured 233 blocks in Budapest this day.

The following day, 6 January, there were no battles on the Buda bank. In central Pest, the 30th Rifle Corps continued to fight for Zugló, and Soviet troops approached Rákosrendező Railway Station. The Germans launched several unsuccessful attacks to cut off the Soviet troops advancing towards the city centre. The Romanian VII Army Corps did not make any significant progress this day, and nor did the 18th Guards Rifle Corps as it had to repel 11 German and Hungarian counter-attacks. Yet, all of Kőbánya was now under Soviet control; the Soviets proceeded to attack Ferencváros, and the 68th Guards Rifle Division also broke into Kispest along Üllő Road.

Soviet riflemen in Csepel. The island was given up by the Germans without a fight to avoid their troops being cut off at one end. (Fortepan, 175235)

The Soviet 17th Air Army did not fly any missions over Budapest on the 6th. The 5th Air Army attacked central Pert in 104 missions during the night, and by day, Il-2 fighters attacked southern Pest and supported the 18th Guards Rifle Corps in 80 missions, A-20 Boston light bombers flew two missions, and Soviet fighters completed a dozen missions with two Il-2s lost. On the Axis side, Soviet shelling and poor weather prevented the Budapest Supply Staff from flying.

Soviet and Romanian forces captured 173 blocks in Budapest on 6 January. In Pest, due to the deep incursions by the Soviets, Pfeffer-Wildenbruch planned to pull back further as the front line was now over-extended and could no longer be held. The airfield in northern Csepel Island was now within Soviet artillery range and unusable: supply would now be via airdrop.

On 7 January, in Buda, the Soviets attacked in Farkasréti Cemetery but the German defenders successfully repelled it. No other fighting took place on the Buda side.

In Pest, the Soviet 30th Rifle Corps continued the fight for Zugló, attempting to capture blocks held by the Germans,

Soviet 120mm mortars preparing to fire on the Weiss Manfréd Factory in the Csepel district of the city. (MTI Photo Archives, F_R19850610009)

who launched nine counter-attacks. They managed to capture 30 blocks over the day. The Romanian VII Army Corps captured 32 blocks in Törökőr, losing a total of 126 troops. The Soviet 18th Guards Rifle Corps faced 20 counter-attacks with tank-support by the defenders this day. The 297th and 66th Rifle divisions were reinforced with a flame-thrower battalion. The fighting for control over Kispest and Pestszenterzsébet continued. The 66th Rifle Division reached the eastern edge of Népliget.

Soviet and Romanian forces captured 173 blocks in Budapest this day. Pfeffer-Wildenbruch was in an ever more difficult situation at the Pest bridgehead, and the 4,000 wounded troops in the pocket could not be evacuated by plane. The IX SS-Mountain Corps had lost 5,600 troops since 25 December, and the supply situation was becoming critical.

On 8 January, Soviet troops managed to take Remete and Látó hills in Buda, but the Hungarian Academy students managed to hold out in their restaurant strongpoint. Óbuda Island was captured by the Soviets without a fight. The Soviets also managed to capture a few blocks to the east of Farkasréti Cemetery.

In Pest, the 30th Rifle Corps fought on to take Zugló. The Soviet 36th Guards Rifle Division was already nearing Hungária Boulevard, the Romanian VII Army Corps captured several blocks in Törökőr, and the whole of Új Lóversenytér airfield was now also under Romanian control. The 18th Guards Rifle Corps reached the barracks on Üllői Avenue but was unable to take them. The Soviet 66th Rifle Division was now entering Népliget, and the 317th was fighting in Kispest. However, the German 22nd SS-Volunteer Cavalry Division still held its positions in Pestszenterzsébet in the face of all the Soviet attacks.

A further 130 blocks were taken in Budapest on the 8th. Pfeffer-Wildenbruch shortened the 22nd SS-Volunteer Cavalry Division's front in Pest to prevent it being surrounded. This meant forfeiting the rest of Csepel Island, and the SS-Cavalry retreated to the northern edge of Kispest and Pestszenterzsébet.

On 9 January, there were no battles on the Buda bank. In Pest, the Soviet 30th Rifle Corps broke into the perimeters of Rákosrendező Railway Station in Zugló. The Germans launched five counter-attacks to recapture the station, but the Soviets repelled all these. The first Soviet riflemen now infiltrated Városliget Park. German and Hungarian forces launched another counter-attack against Új Lóversenytér airfield, but could not retake it. Romanian forces also now began attacking the barracks on Üllői Avenue.

The battles here were so intense that one of the Romanian platoons was left with only five uninjured troops by evening. The Soviet 18th Guards Rifle Corps also joined in, and captured areas to the east of Kerepesi Cemetery, as well as eastern areas of Józsefváros Railway Station. They also secured the whole of Népliget. In southern Pest, the Soviets gained (abandoned) Kispest and Pestszentlőrinc uncontested, and secured 470 blocks. In northern Csepel Island, they took more than 700 prisoners, and looted the factories, eight ammunition depots, 100 freight wagons and a fuel depot there.

With the Soviets now at Rákosrendező Railway Station, Pfeffer-Wildenbruch feared German forces in northern Pest might be surrounded, and pulled back the front line to Rákos Creek, vacating Újpest and Pestújhely that night.

On 10 January, there was no combat on the Buda bank. In Pest, the 30th Soviet Rifle Corps secured Újpest and Pestújhely. However, they could not pass the defences at Magdolnaváros Railway Station. During the day, Soviet forces repelled three German counter-attacks at the station, and eventually captured it by the end of the day. The 30th Rifle Corps also managed to break through the defences of the Railway Ring and into Városliget Park, and a battle of multiple waves ensued. German and Hungarian forces launched several counter-attacks, with even Hungarian police troops deployed in Ansaldo armoured cars, yet the Soviets kept their foothold in the park. The Romanian VII Army Corps reached Hungária Boulevard and continued the fight for the Üllői Avenua barracks, capturing 117 prisoners but losing 140 troops on the 10th. The Soviet 18th Guards Rifle Corps infiltrated Kerepesi Cemetery, achieving yet another deep breach. After clearing up in Népliget, they continued towards Orczy Garden. The Germans launched several unsuccessful counter-attacks against the Soviets near Kerepesi Cemetery and Népliget. The Soviets were now at some parts of Könyves Kálmán Boulevard. In total, some 1,000 blocks were secured in Budapest on this day.

On 11 January, the Soviet General Staff attempted to centralize the siege command. Malinovsky, however, did not wholly go along with this. He thought that eliminating the Buda bridgehead was Tolbukhin's responsibility, and thus the Budapest Group was set up independently in Pest, comprising the staff of the Soviet 18th Rifle Corps, tasked with coordinating the operations of about 11 divisions in Pest. To crush the remnants of the Pest bridgehead, Malinovsky set simple objectives: the 30th Rifle Corps was to reach Széchenyi Chain Bridge, and the 18th Guards Rifle Corps the Ferenc József Bridge (thus bisecting the bridgehead) by 14 January.

On 11 January, once again the Buda bank of the Danube remained quiet. In Pest, the 30th Soviet Rifle Corps, reinforced with flame-throwers, crossed Rákos Creek and entered Angyalföld. Fighting continued in Városliget Park, most of which fell, with the battles now focusing on its western end, and Soviet troops also crossed Dózsa György Road. The Romanian VII Army Corps continued to besiege Üllői Avenue barracks, and also advanced

The pillars of the Chain Bridge, with the Royal Castle in the background. The Germans demolished the Chain Bridge and Erzsébet Bridge last, on 18 January 1945, after evacuating the Pest bridgehead. (Fortepan, 175162)

towards Keleti Railway Station. The Soviet 18th Guards Rifle Corps, together with the Romanians, reached the southern parts of Kerepes Cemetery, and entered its perimeter for the night by blowing a hole in the cemetery wall. They also completed the capture of Józsefváros Railway Station. Their forces then continued west, north of Üllői Avenue, to secure Orczy Square briefly until half of it was retaken with an Axis counter-attack. The Soviets managed to reach Könyves Kálmán Boulevard along its whole length, and crossed it in several locations. Soviet and Romanian forces captured 150 blocks in Budapest on this day.

Soviet artillery in Hősök (Heroes') Square, with the ruined Millennial Monument in the background. (MTI Photo Archives, F_S_31080)

On 12 January, with *Konrad II* aborted, the fighting in Buda also intensified. In central Buda, the Germans launched two counter-attacks and managed to capture the BBTE Sports Ground. Meanwhile, the Soviet 108th Guards Rifle Division assaulted Kis-Sváb Hill, but were repulsed. The Soviet 320th Rifle Division planned to eliminate the Sas Hill defences by surrounding then liquidating them. The 320th Rifle Division launched an attack in Kelenföld to capture its remaining enemy-held parts before moving to the north of the Lágymányos Railway Embankment. They made very little progress for the loss of 50 troops. The 83rd Naval Infantry Brigade attacked the Lágymányos Railway Embankment at Budafoki Road, crossed it, but the attack then stalled, and they had to return to their starting positions in the evening.

In Pest, the Germans withdrew from Angyalföld. The Soviet 30th Rifle Corps continued its slow advance towards Nagykörút Boulevard, but secured Városliget Park, eliminating the remaining resistance hotspots, and Hősök Square. The Romanian VII Army Corps was also moving slowly towards Keleti Railway Station, while Üllői Avenue barracks was still holding out. In Kerepes Cemetery, the fighting was so intense that the Romanian 19th Infantry Division lost 115 troops on this day. The Soviet 18th Guards Rifle Corps took the cemetery, but a German–Hungarian counter-attack recaptured half of it during the day. The Soviets slowly advanced towards Nagykörút Boulevard. Soviet and Romanian forces captured 135 blocks in Budapest on the 12th.

On 13 January, the Soviet 108th Guards Rifle Division recaptured the BBTE Sports Ground, lost the day before, but they could not get past the Botanical Research Institute and the Baár-Madas Grammar School, and the attack lost momentum here. The Soviet 108th Guards Rifle Division tried once again to capture Kis-Sváb Hill. The defenders repelled the attack, but the Soviets managed to capture three buildings used as outposts. The 83rd Naval Infantry Brigade received 144 reinforcement troops and strong artillery support, but their attack on the Lágymányos Railway Embankment still failed to bring results. In Farkasréti Cemetery, the Soviets attacked with assault gun support and advanced a few hundred metres before they were halted. The northeastern tip of the cemetery remained under Axis control.

In Pest, the Soviet 30th Rifle Corps continued to attack from Angyalföld towards Nyugati Railway Station and Nagykörút Boulevard. Városliget Park was almost wholly under Soviet control, but the attack bogged down

An AT obstacle made of railway track near Erzsébet Bridge on Eskü Road (today known as Szabadsajtó Road). (Fortepan, 60158)

in Erzsébetváros district. The Romanian VII Army Corps finally cleared the Üllői Avenue barracks, capturing 497 prisoners during these several days of fighting. The Romanians were now already attacking Keleti Railway Station, where they faced a barricade built from railway carriages. They were only able to enter the station with Soviet support, and only managed to secure part of it. A German counter-attack unsuccessfully attempted to eject them from the building. The Soviet 18th Guards Rifle Corps finished clearing Kerepes Cemetery, then took cenral Ferencváros and reached Nagykörút Boulevard.

On 14 January in Buda, the Soviet 108th Guards Rifle Division assaulted the fortified Baár-Madas Grammar School and the Botanical Research Institute, but both held out. The Soviets lost two SP guns during a German counter-attack. The Soviet 320th Rifle Division managed to capture the barracks south of Sas Hill. German and Hungarian forces launched a counter-attack to end the Soviet incursion but to no avail. The Soviet attack to take Farkasréti Cemetery failed. The fighting in Kelenföld continued, but the Soviets were unable to advance on the northern side of the Lágymányos Railway Embankment due to the well-placed defences in the neighbouring houses. The 83rd Naval Infantry Brigade's attack against the Lágymányos Railway Embankment failed again.

In Pest, the Soviet 30th Rifle Corps took 70 blocks. Angyalföld was fully under Soviet control, and the freight terminal of Nyugati Railway Station was also taken. The Romanian VII Army Corps cleared Keleti Railway Station, and the Soviet 18th Guards Rifle Corps reached Nagykörút Boulevard in several places, and crossed it towards Kálvin Square. A total of 94 blocks in Budapest were taken on this day.

On 15 January, in Buda, the Soviet 320th Rifle Division assaulted Sas Hill from the west, taking the summit, but a German–Hungarian counter-attack, supported by assault guns, surrounded a battalion-size group of Soviet troops there and they remained cut off for a day. Soviet troops also attacked Márton Hill, north of Farkasréti Cemetery, taking most of it, apart from a few buildings. The 320th was reinforced with assault rifles, flame-throwers and artillery, then continued its attack north of the Lágymányos Railway Embankment, but managed to capture only a few buildings.

A Soviet 25mm 72-K air-defence gun in Pest. (MTI Photo Archives, F_RAS19840730066)

In Pest, the Germans attempted to retake Keleti Railway Station, but then retreated to Nagykörút Boulevard. It had previously been readied for defence, with 2–3m-deep and 1–2m-high barricades made out of burnt-out tram carriages and furniture blocking the side streets and cobblestone barricades at the main junctions. In addition, eight rows of barbed-wire cut the main roads leading to the boulevard, with one row comprising high-voltage electric wire. Mines had also been hidden in squares and major junctions, and fire positions established in corner buildings.

The Soviet 30th Rifle Corps captured 152 blocks this day and closed in on a sizeable stretch of Nagykörút Boulevard. They invaded Újlipótváros and the battle for Nyugati Railway Station began. The Romanian VII Army Corps was withdrawn from the front line on the 15th, playing their final part in the battles for Budapest. The Soviet 18th Guards Rifle Corps reached Kálvin Square and crossed Nagykörút Boulevard at all points in their zone.

Planting of the Soviet flag on top of the New York Palace in Pest, January 1945. The main thoroughfare of Nagykörút Boulevard can be seen in the lower centre of the picture. (Fortepan, 175132)

Soviet and Romanian forces captured 200 blocks in Budapest on the 15th. Pfeffer-Wildenbruch now realized that the Pest bridgehead would not last long, and its evacuation was inevitable. The Germans demolished Horthy Miklós Bridge the same day.

On 16 January, in Buda, the Soviet 108th Guards Rifle Division attempted to capture Kis-Sváb Hill. They managed to seize a small part of the hill, but the defenders still held the summit. The Soviet 320th Rifle Division again attacked at Farkasréti Cemetery, but only managed to secure its south-eastern area. The Soviets did manage to finish taking Márton Hill, and the Soviet group surrounded on Sas Hill was also rescued. A team of the 83rd Naval Infantry Brigade set out to bypass the defenders of the Lágymányos Railway Embankment by passing through a canal under the embankment, but several troops lost consciousness in the oxygen-poor environment. Subsequent medical examinations revealed that 31 of the team's 55 troops were not even fit for battlefield service. To the north of the embankment, along Karolina Road, fighting again flared up. The Soviets attacked with armoured support, losing one tank, but could not break through. The Germans fortified the defences with AT guns.

Stray horses roaming the streets of Pest in January 1945. Horsemeat was an essential food source for both civilians and soldiers during the siege, preventing many from starving to death. (MTI Photo Archives, 753030)

In Pest, the Soviet 30th Rifle Corps repelled three German counter-attacks, then captured Nyugati Railway Station and reached Nagykörút Boulevard along its whole length. The 18th Guards Rifle Corps continued westwards in central Pest.

Hitler granted Pfeffer-Wildenbruch full powers in regard to the Pest bridgehead. Its evacuation began during daylight on the 16th, across bridges under constant attack. The Germans blew up Ferenc József Bridge on this day.

On 17 January, in Buda, the Soviet 320th Rifle Division launched another attack on Sas Hill from the west and set on fire a few building strongpoints but did not achieve a major breakthrough for the loss of 42 troops. The Soviet attack in Farkasréti Cemetery was also repelled. The Soviets managed to capture

ABOVE LEFT
The ruins of Erzsébet Bridge, which was destroyed by the Germans. (Fortepan, 52044)

ABOVE RIGHT
Soviet troops plant the Red Flag in front of the entrance to the Parliament Building on 18 January 1945. The building was used as an emergency hospital, and was occupied by the Soviets without a fight. (Fortepan, 175231)

a block north of the Lágymányos Railway Embankment and reached Karolina Road.

In Pest, the Soviet 30th Rifle Corps failed to cross Nagykörút Boulevard to the west of Nyugati Railway Station, but to the east they penetrated deeper into the city – several Hungarian units surrendered in this zone, and the Soviets thus managed to cross the Nagykörút. The Soviet 18th Guards Rifle Corps reached Kiskörút Boulevard. The Germans continued counter-attacking, which slowed the Soviet advance.

On 18 January, in Buda, the Soviets managed to cross Karolina Road and capture another block north of the Lágymányos Railway Embankment. A platoon of the Vannay Battalion arrived to strengthen the Axis defences in Farkasréti Cemetery, and the defenders repelled a further Soviet attack.

The Soviet 25th Guards Rifle Division managed to cross the river unnoticed to the northern tip of Margit Island, and establish a bridgehead around the pillars of the later Árpád Bridge, still under construction at the time.

In Pest, the Germans demolished the Széchenyi Chain Bridge and the Erzsébet Bridge in the morning after evacuating the bridgehead the previous night. The Soviet troops pushed forward towards the Parliament, and took it without resistance. The building served as an emergency hospital, and was hit by 8,250 mortar rounds, 300 incendiary bombs and 30 larger shells during the fighting. Many Hungarian troops no longer wished to move to Buda and continue the fight, and instead stayed in Pest with the intent of surrendering. According to Soviet sources, Soviet forces captured 18,000 prisoners of war on this day. The fight for the Pest bridgehead was over.

GERMAN RELIEF OPERATIONS: *KONRAD I–III*

When Budapest was surrounded, Hitler, in agreement with General Heinz Guderian (chief of staff of all German land forces in the East), ordered the IV SS-Panzer Corps (stationed in Poland as a reserve) to Hungary to restore connection to Budapest. This move had little effect on the outcome of the Soviet Vistula-Oder Offensive launched later, in January 1945, as the Soviets had more than five times the Germans in terms of both manpower and tanks, and more than ten times the aircraft; the corps's presence would not majorly affect these ratios.

The German plans assumed that the Soviet troops west of Budapest were still on the move and solid defence lines were not yet established.

Also, the 3rd Ukrainian Front had been worn down by heavy fighting, with earlier losses not yet replaced. In terms of reinforcements, Soviet forces in occupied Poland had precedence over those in Hungary. The Soviet divisions stood at around 50–60 per cent strength. Moreover, Soviet reconnaissance had misplaced the location of the upcoming German attack – it indicated the area of Székesfehérvár to be the starting point of the German counter-offensive.

The IV SS-Panzer Corps, under *SS-Gruppenführer* Herbert Otto Gille, consisted of the 3rd SS-Panzer Division Totenkopf, the 5th SS-Panzer

A pair of StuG III assault guns advance on Budapest during Operation *Konrad III*. (Süddeutsche Zeitung/Alamy)

Division Wiking, as well as the 96th and 711th Infantry divisions attached as reinforcements. The strength of the attacking German forces was 63,000 troops, with fighting strength probably much lower. The Germans had a total of 285 tanks, assault guns and panzerjägers. These included nine Tigers, 112 Panthers, 57 Panzer IVs, 55 Jagdpanzer IVs and 35 StuG IV units.

Two plans were drawn up for the relief effort, without Hitler's interference. The first did indeed begin near Székesfehérvár and head towards Budapest on flat terrain – the so-called *Südlösung*, or 'Southern Solution', also known as Operation *Paula*. The other planned offensive started at Komárom and proceeded through wooded, mountainous terrain, where the Germans had limited room for manoeuvre with their panzers, and, at the same time, the Soviets had better defence options – this was the so-called *Nordlösung*, or 'Northern Solution', also known as Operation *Konrad*. Of the two, the Germans chose the latter, with a major factor in the decision being that the distance to be travelled to Budapest was less, and the plan required 900m^3 less fuel for the offensive than *Paula*. Originally, the offensive was scheduled for 31 December, but as neither fuel nor ammunition had arrived in sufficient quantities by then, it was postponed to 1 January 1945.

The attack needed to be launched as soon as possible, before the Soviets could organize their defences. From the outset, there were questions over whether there would be sufficient infantry presence to support the attack. In addition, adequate air support was also a precondition for the success of the German armoured attacks. Destroying the Soviet defences was mainly up to the German assault aircraft, and without such capacities, the attackers would be forced to destroy these at heavy cost and losses. At the same time, the Soviets had significant reserves despite the 3rd Ukrainian Front's fatigued state. In the zone of the German offensive, the Soviet 4th Guards Army was on the defence. It had 280 AT guns, with half of these assigned to 39 AT groups. In addition, the 18th Tank Corps and the 2nd Guards Mechanized Corps were positioned behind the 4th Guards Army, and these, together, had more than 200 tanks and assault guns, including 152 T-34s.

Konrad I

The IV SS-Panzer Corps's transfer to Hungary was to be executed by 1 January 1945 according to plans, but was not wholly completed by then.

Nevertheless, on 1 January, at 1930hrs, the 3rd SS-Panzer Division and the 711th Infantry Division began their assault along the Danube. At the same time, the 96th Infantry Division crossed the Danube and created a bridgehead in the area of Nyergesújfalu and Süttő. Also, the 5th SS-Panzer Division attacked from Tata. This comprised the main thrust of the offensive. The assault surprised the Soviet 31st Guards Rifle Corps: the Germans broke through its line and advanced 20–30km deep, possibly also surprising other Soviet forces still being deployed. The Germans bypassed and surrounded the AT concentrations. However, due to bad weather, the German 4th Air Fleet was only able to carry out 100 missions in support of the attack on this day.

On 2 January, the Germans took Nyergesújfalu and Tardos. The Soviets tried to leverage their air superiority to slow the German offensive, and the forces attacking Budapest gave up their AT reserves to the 4th Guards Army, located in the path of *Konrad*, and the 2nd Ukrainian Front also transferred some artillery. In addition, AT mines were laid in 54 locations. With the newly arriving reinforcements, the Soviets established a line of defence in the zone between Zsámbék and Bicske, and further strengthened it with the 1st Guards Mechanized Corps and the 18th Tank Corps. The German 4th Air Fleet, together with Hungarian air forces, flew 360 missions in support of the offensive.

The German assault reached the Bicske–Zsámbék area on 4 January, and also neared Szomor, Csolnok and Esztergom. This day, IV SS-Panzer Corps reported having destroyed or captured 79 tanks, 160 artillery pieces and 107 AT guns, and the air forces reported having destroyed 50 tanks, 17 AT guns and 87 aircraft. Despite these successes, the German attack was halted by the Soviet defences between Zsámbék and Bicske. The Soviets, having directed their reinforcements here, established their defences here at a depth of 4–5km, with three AT zones, each with 40–50 AT guns.

On 5 January, one of the SS-Panzer-Grenadier regiments was tasked with breaching the Soviet defences, neutralizing Soviet camouflaged AT weapons and dug-in tanks around Csabdi and Mány, but their attack failed. They could not take Csabdi, and only managed to reach Hegyikastély on the Bicske–Mány road in the area of Mány.

On 6 January, the Germans launched another attack against Csabdi, but their armoured *Kampfgruppe* Darges was surrounded at Hegyikastély by the Soviets, and they had to fight encircled for days. They repelled dozens of Soviet attacks, sometimes at close quarters. Though the Germans eventually succeeded in capturing Csabdi and relieving their surrounded troops at Hegyikastély, their attack lost momentum. They were unable to get past the Soviet defensive line and reach Budapest. On 6 January, they managed to reach and take Esztergom on the Danube, but the offensive abated. The IV SS-Panzer Corps suffered heavy losses between 1 and 7 January, totalling 3,500 troops (including 530 dead) and 39 AFVs.

Meanwhile, on 6 January, the Soviets launched a relief attack from Garam, north

SS-Panzer-Grenadiers in SdKfz 251s pass the remains of a Soviet column during Operation *Konrad III*. (Süddeutsche Zeitung/Alamy)

of the Danube, in the direction of Komárom. They achieved a significant breakthrough, but then became stuck in the German defences before Komárom; after 10 January, the unfolding German counter-attack stabilized the situation.

Konrad II

The Germans wanted to proceed with the attack halted in the Zsámbék–Bicske zone by regrouping units to another location and deploying new forces. Thus evolved Operation *Konrad II*. The 5th SS-Panzer Division regrouped at Esztergom, and was given orders to reach Budapest via the Pilis Hills. In parallel, the Germans also launched an attack near Székesfehérvár, and their forces in the Zsámbék–Bicske zone continued trying to break through the defence line.

On 6 January, the German 3rd and 23rd Panzer divisions, the Hungarian 2nd Armoured Division and the German 4th Cavalry Brigade, departing from Mór, attacked towards Zámoly and Csákvár with the aim of reaching Bicske, thus cutting off the Soviet supply lines that the previous attack between Mány and Zsámbék had severed, before reaching Budapest via Budaörs.

The Soviet 32nd Guards Rifle Corps and the 68th Rifle Corps had established a well-built defensive system with strong AT artillery and reserves. The Soviets were well aware of where the attack would come from. It was launched on the morning of 7 January, with a brief preparatory artillery bombardment and Luftwaffe support, but no decisive breakthrough was achieved. The Germans launched several attacks in the days that followed, but these were all neutralized by Soviet counter-attacks. On 7 January, the Germans took Sárkereszt, then on the 9th they approached Zámoly. Here a minor armour battle unfolded , with the Germans reporting having destroyed 68 Soviet AFVs in a single day. After a battle of changing fortunes, the Germans managed to capture Zámoly on 11 January, but with this, the attack waned. They managed to infiltrate some Soviet positions and inflict heavy losses, but achieved no breakthrough. Meanwhile, along the Bicske–Zsámbék line, the German attacks continued, but other than taking Csabdi on the 7th, they achieved nothing.

To the north, near Esztergom, the offensive was executed by two *kampfgruppen*. *Kampfgruppe* Philipp, comprising the reinforced II./284th Panzer-Grenadier Regiment, five tanks and assault guns, six infantry fighting vehicles and three armoured vehicles. According to the plans, the *Kampfgruppe* Philipp, together with the German 96th Infantry Division, was to advance to Budapest along the Danube and ensure that supplies could reach the capital via the opened route. The other was *Kampfgruppe* Westland, comprising the SS-Panzer-Grenadier Regiment 'Westland', an armoured pioneer battalion, an armoured artillery division, a field artillery division, a panzerjäger division and an armoured reconnaissance division. *Kampfgruppe* Westland, together with the German 711th Infantry Division, was to attack from Gyarmatpuszta on 9 January, then cross the Pilis Mountains heading for Pomáz and Szentendre, where they were to join *Kampfgruppe* Philipp. German forces breaking out of Budapest were also to head for this area, establishing the link-up. However, Hitler vetoed the Budapest breakout, and the offensive thus began on 10 January without it.

Kampfgruppe Philipp's attack progressed much slower than planned, and stalled at Pilismarót. *Kampfgruppe* Westland did significantly better and reached Pilisszentlélek, and on 11 January, also managed to take

Pilisszentkereszt, from where the lights of Budapest could be seen. They also reached the field hospital in nearby Dobogókő, where they freed the German and Hungarian wounded troops held there. At this point, however, Hitler intervened and ordered both *kampfgruppen* to halt their further attacks. The flanks of *Kampfgruppe* Westland were only about 20km from Budapest at this point, but even if they managed to break through, they would have to secure a route through the hills.

Konrad III

Having lost faith in the 'northern' attack, Hitler turned his attention to implementing the previously rejected 'southern' option. The original plans were redrawn, and given the code name *Konrad III*. The objectives were now much greater. The attack starting from Székesfehérvár would skirt south of Lake Velence and reach the Danube, before turning north and reaching Budapest, surrounding Soviet forces west of the city. Surprise and speed were crucial elements of the plan, reaching the Danube as quickly as possible.

For the offensive, the forces of *Konrad I* were redeployed near Székesfehérvár. The attack was originally assigned to a regrouped and reinforced German IV SS-Panzer Corps, comprising the 1st and 3rd Panzer divisions, the 3rd and 5th SS-Panzer divisions, and the 23rd Panzer Division (III Panzer Corps) and the German 4th Cavalry Brigade. However, there were now no infantry divisions supporting the attack. The redeployment order was issued on 12 January, and executed in darkness. At this time the Soviets were launching the Vistula-Oder Offensive, and Soviet intelligence thought that any German forces withdrawn would be sent to the Vistula. Bad weather also hindered Soviet air reconnaissance operations, and the Soviets thus could not make accurate predictions.

An SdKfz 250 of 5th SS-Panzer Division Wiking during Operation *Konrad III* on 20 January 1945. (Süddeutsche Zeitung/Alamy)

On the Soviet side, a layered defence system was established by the 20th and the 21st Guard Rifle corps, heavily reinforced with obstacles (including AT and anti-personnel mines, and electric barriers). The Soviet 7th Mechanized Corps was also available as a reserve.

The Germans launched their attack on the morning of 18 January, following a short preparatory artillery bombardment between Lake Balaton and Vértes Mountains. The attack came as a huge surprise to the Soviet side, and the Germans managed to break through the defences on the first day. Yet, eliminating the Soviet AT zones and obstacles forced the attackers to a temporary halt, thus slowing German progress. The Germans captured Enying and Polgárdi on this day, broke through the Soviet defences in depth, reached Sárvíz Canal and approached Székesfehérvár, and also captured Simontornya and Sáregres. However, they did not manage to capture the bridges across Sárvíz Canal, as these were demolished by the Soviets, and the Germans only managed to establish a number of bridgeheads over the canal. On the first day, the Germans broke through the Soviet positions on a 20km-wide front. Meanwhile, the Soviets began deploying their reinforcement forces, and the 18th Tank

Corps was moved forward to strengthen the defences.

The German 4th Air Fleet flew 270 missions over the area on the 18th, and 12 Soviet aircraft were reported shot down. Due to the unfolding German attack, the Soviet air divisions were forced to relocate east of the Danube, to avoid air attack. This extra distance reduced their efficiency. On the first day, the Germans inflicted heavy losses, destroying 80 AT guns, as well as 11 tanks and 20 SP guns, but they themselves also suffered heavy losses.

On 19 January, the Soviets attacked the German bridgeheads established the day before on the eastern bank of Sárvíz Canal but the Germans repelled the attacks, then rebuilt the bridges. The Germans then broke out of the bridgeheads. They actually breached the front line of the 3rd Ukrainian Front, causing panic among the Soviet units who fled to the Danube crossing points, abandoning their weapons. The Germans reached the Danube and took Dunapentele. The staff of the 3rd Ukrainian Front was not far from here, in Dunaföldvár, and the Germans could easily have captured them as there were no other Soviet forces available in the area.

A Panther moves through a Hungarian village on the road to Budapest during Operation *Konrad III* on 20 January 1945. (Süddeutsche Zeitung/Alamy)

Heavy fighting unfolded around Perkáta and Seregélyes as the Soviet 133rd Rifle Corps and the 18th Tank Corps moved up; the Germans eventually managed to surround these units, but lacked sufficient infantry to liquidate them. The ice on the Danube was beginning to break up, making Soviet reinforcement and regrouping across the pontoon bridges impossible. For this reason, Soviet reinforcements were flown in. To stabilize the situation, the Soviet 5th Guards Cavalry Corps, parts of the 1st Guards Mechanized Corps and artillery regiments reassigned from the 2nd Ukrainian Front were deployed between Lake Velence and the Danube. The German 4th Air Fleet was hindered by bad weather, yet they managed to fly 270 missions, and at least 20 Soviet aircraft were reported shot down.

The Germans were now facing a dilemma: either destroy the surrounded Soviet units and forfeit the advantage of speed, allowing the arriving Soviet 5th Guards Cavalry Corps to build up defences between Lake Velence and the Danube; or continue the offensive towards Budapest. At this point, the lack of infantry was proving a major hindrance, preventing the liquidation of the surrounded Soviet units. The Germans decided to continue the attack towards Budapest.

On 20 January, the Germans captured Agárd, Gárdony, Perkáta and parts of Pusztaszabolcs, then continued along the Danube, and took Rácalmás and Kulcs. Meanwhile, the Soviet 5th Guards Cavalry Corps arrived and managed to establish a 7–8km-deep defensive zone between Lake Velence and the Danube. The Soviet 1st Guards Mechanized Corps also arrived and its two mechanized brigades reinforced the cavalry corps with 133 AFVs.

On 21 January, the surrounded troops of the Soviet 133rd Rifle Corps and 18th Tank Corps (which had lost half of its tanks) broke out to the south, towards Hercegfalva. Meanwhile, the Germans continued to push

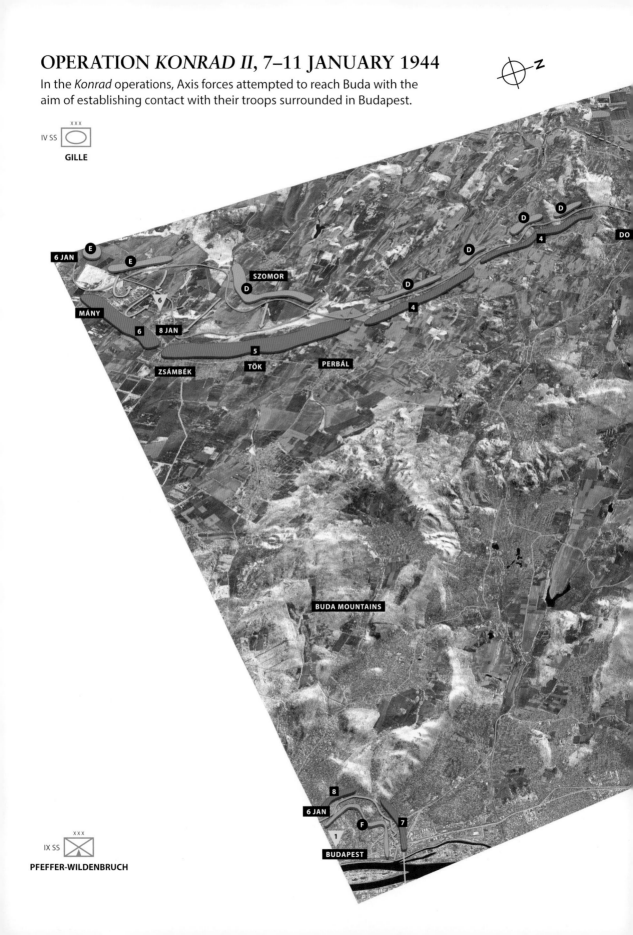

OPERATION *KONRAD II*, 7–11 JANUARY 1944

In the *Konrad* operations, Axis forces attempted to reach Buda with the
aim of establishing contact with their troops surrounded in Budapest.

IV SS ⬭ GILLE

SZOMOR

6 JAN

MÁNY

8 JAN

ZSÁMBÉK

TÖK

PERBÁL

DO

BUDA MOUNTAINS

6 JAN

BUDAPEST

IX SS ⊠ PFEFFER-WILDENBRUCH

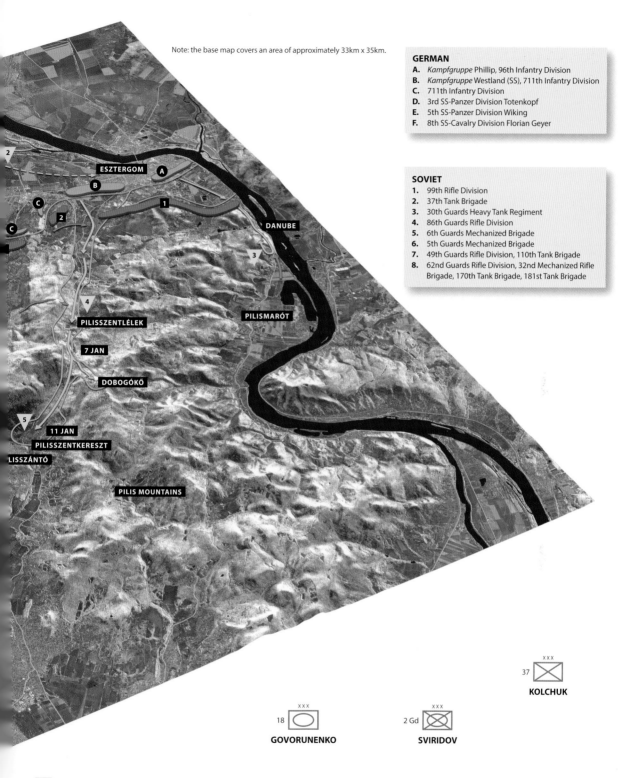

Note: the base map covers an area of approximately 33km x 35km.

GERMAN
A. *Kampfgruppe* Phillip, 96th Infantry Division
B. *Kampfgruppe* Westland (SS), 711th Infantry Division
C. 711th Infantry Division
D. 3rd SS-Panzer Division Totenkopf
E. 5th SS-Panzer Division Wiking
F. 8th SS-Cavalry Division Florian Geyer

SOVIET
1. 99th Rifle Division
2. 37th Tank Brigade
3. 30th Guards Heavy Tank Regiment
4. 86th Guards Rifle Division
5. 6th Guards Mechanized Brigade
6. 5th Guards Mechanized Brigade
7. 49th Guards Rifle Division, 110th Tank Brigade
8. 62nd Guards Rifle Division, 32nd Mechanized Rifle Brigade, 170th Tank Brigade, 181st Tank Brigade

ESZTERGOM

DANUBE

PILISSZENTLÉLEK

7 JAN

PILISMARÓT

DOBOGÓKŐ

11 JAN
PILISSZENTKERESZT
LISSZÁNTÓ

PILIS MOUNTAINS

18 GOVORUNENKO

2 Gd SVIRIDOV

37 KOLCHUK

EVENTS

1. 8 January 1945: Hitler refuses to allow the IX SS-Mountain Corps to break out towards the Pilis Mountains to support the relief forces.

2. 9 January 1945: Part of the 5th SS-Panzer Division is reassigned to Esztergom.

3. 10 January 1945: The attack by *Kampfgruppe* Philipp reaches the vicinity of Pilismarót, but further advances are prevented by Soviet forces.

4. *Kampfgruppe* Westland succeeds in breaching the Soviet positions and advances to Pilisszentlélek in the Pilis Mountains.

5. Evening, 11 January 1945: *Kampfgruppe* Westland takes Pilisszentkereszt, but Hitler vetos further advances.

6. Further German attacks take place against the Soviet defences established on the line Bicske–Zsámbék (this map only shows the area between Mány and Zsámbék), but the Germans make only modest advances, and fail to breach the Soviet defences.

Operation *Konrad III*, 18–27 January 1945

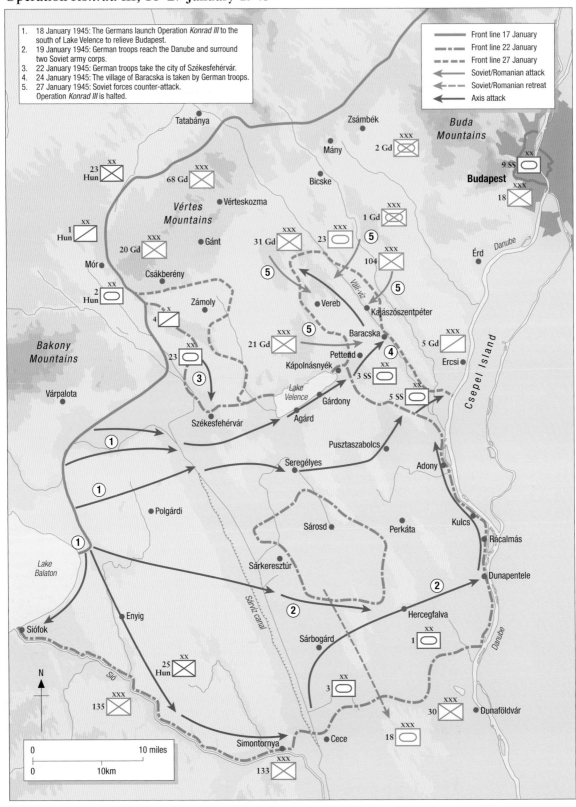

1. 18 January 1945: The Germans launch Operation *Konrad III* to the south of Lake Velence to relieve Budapest.
2. 19 January 1945: German troops reach the Danube and surround two Soviet army corps.
3. 22 January 1945: German troops take the city of Székesfehérvár.
4. 24 January 1945: The village of Baracska is taken by German troops.
5. 27 January 1945: Soviet forces counter-attack. Operation *Konrad III* is halted.

Front line 17 January
Front line 22 January
Front line 27 January
Soviet/Romanian attack
Soviet/Romanian retreat
Axis attack

Tatabánya
Zsámbék
Buda Mountains
Mány
2 Gd
Budapest
9 SS
23 Hun
68 Gd
Bicske
18
Vértes Mountains
Vérteskozma
1 Gd
1 Hun
Gánt
31 Gd
23
104
Érd
Danube
20 Gd
Mór
Csákberény
Vereb
2 Hun
Zámoly
Kajászószentpéter
4
21 Gd
Baracska
5 Gd
23
Pettend
Ercsi
Kápolnásnyék
3 SS
Bakony Mountains
Lake Velence
5 SS
Várpalota
Gárdony
Székesfehérvár
Agárd
Csepel Island
Pusztaszabolcs
Seregélyes
Adony
Polgárdi
Sárosd
Perkáta
Kulcs
Rácalmás
Lake Balaton
Sárkeresztúr
Dunapentele
Sárvíz canal
Enyig
Hercegfalva
Siófok
1
Sárbogárd
N
25 Hun
3
Sió
135
30
Dunaföldvár
Simontornya
Cece
18
0   10 miles
0   10km
133

64

north towards Budapest, capturing Adony. However, the attacking German 3rd Panzer Division had to pull back to Hercegfalva to deal with the Soviet forces that appeared in their rear, avoiding encirclement. The Germans also managed to capture Pusztaszabolcs on this day in a lengthy battle. However, they failed to cross the area between Lake Velence and the Danube to the north, as the Soviet defences were now fully established. The German 4th Air Fleet flew 100 attack-support missions, but the Soviet air forces played only a limited role in the fighting on the 21st.

That evening, the German 1st Panzer Division launched a general assault to take Székesfehérvár, achieving this the following morning. They captured 800 Soviet prisoners in the town and a huge amount of materiel, including American Studebaker trucks, Hanomag tractors and Opel Blitz trucks, as well as 40 tanks, including the German panzers previously captured by the Soviets. These items were redeployed in the fighting that followed.

On 22 January, the Germans continued attacking towards Budapest; they captured Iváncsa, crossed Váli Creek and established a bridgehead. Near Hercegfalva, they inflicted further losses on the Soviet units breaking out of encirclement. The Germans planned to redeploy their Székesfehérvár forces, now disengaged, along Lake Velence against the Soviet defensive line. In addition, the German Cavalry Corps was to launch a relief attack from the direction of Bicske. The German 4th Air Fleet executed 400 missions, with 31 Soviet aircraft reported shot down, and also attacked the bridge at Dunaföldvár, but with little success. The Soviet air forces flew 1,034 missions, and shot down 36 enemy aircraft.

On 23 January, the German offensive reached Váli Creek, but failed to cross it and move forward. The German Cavalry Corps' attack was only partially successful: it took Mány but could not proceed further. The Soviet 5th Guards Cavalry Corps reported having destroyed 39 tanks this day, for the loss of only three. The German 4th Air Fleet flew 200 missions during daylight, and the same number at night.

On 24 January, the Germans captured parts of Baracska, but still could not cross Váli Creek; they did manage to secure Hercegfalva. The attack along the Danube was also slow going. The forces redeployed from Székesfehérvár tried to proceed from Kápolnásnyék towards Baracska, but only reached Pettend, where their attack lost momentum. Also on the 24th, the German 4th Cavalry Brigade and the Hungarian 2nd Armoured Division launched another attack from Zámoly and Csákberény, but this had only limited results and also petered out. Bad weather prevented the German 4th Air Fleet from flying many missions this day.

On 25 January, the Soviets began preparing their counter-offensive, using recently arrived reinforcements. Despite all their efforts, the Germans had still not taken the bridge over Váli Creek at Baracska, but did manage to capture Pettend in heavy fighting. The German secondary axes of attack achieved limited results, with the capture of Gánt and Vérteskosma. Meanwhile, reinforcements in the form

SS-Panzer-Grenadiers move forward during Operation *Konrad III*, past the bodies of fallen Soviet soldiers, 23 January 1945. (Süddeutsche Zeitung/Alamy)

SS-Panzer-Grenadiers in snow camouflage, fire on Soviet troops during Operation *Konrad III* on 24 January 1945. (Süddeutsche Zeitung/Alamy)

of the Soviet 23rd Tank Corps and the 104th Rifle Corps arrived to join the counter-offensive. The German 4th Air Fleet flew only 60 missions this day due to continuing poor weather, and German air reconnaissance failed to detect the Soviet reinforcements.

Faced with the results to date, the German command modified their original plan. The new plan was to surround and eliminate the Soviet forces north of Lake Velence, attacking from two directions, then continue the offensive towards Budapest.

On 26 January, the Germans renewed their offensive, unaware of the arrival of the Soviet reinforcements. The Germans managed to reach Kajászószentpéter, but even here they were unable to cross Váli Creek. The German forces then turned west, and captured Vereb. Further attack units captured Pázmánd before turning towards Vál, where they also reached Váli Creek, but were unable to proceed. A 10km-deep, 6km-wide salient had been formed, in which the Germans were stuck, unable to advance further.

On 27 January, the Soviet counter-offensive began. The Soviet air forces executed 260 missions in support, but the German 4th Air Fleet aircraft mostly remained grounded due to bad weather. Soviet forces attacked the German salient from all three sides, but were unable to penetrate it. However, the Soviet offensive took the Germans by surprise, and the chances to relieve Budapest evaporated. Hitler ordered Operation *Konrad III* aborted, and German troops withdrew from the salient the following day. Military operations continued until 15 February, but witnessed only gradual Soviet advances at the expense of the Germans: by the end of January, Soviet forces had recaptured Adony, Pusztaszabolcs, Dunapentele, Perkáta and Simontornya, and by 11 February, Zámoly, Seregélyes, Sárkeresztúr and Sárosd.

BUDA: 18 JANUARY–10 FEBRUARY 1945

By evacuating the Pest bridgehead, the German forces defending Buda increased in number, but their fighting strength stood at only 15,000 troops, 11,000 of whom were German. The Axis defensive disposition changed only slightly in consequence: the German 8th SS-Cavalry Division maintained its position, as did the Hungarian units, such as the Vannay Battalion and the Viharos Combat Group. The German 22nd SS-Volunteer Cavalry Division, arriving from Pest, was tasked with protecting the Danube riverbank and Margit Island. What was left of the German 13th Panzer Division and Panzer Division Feldherrnhalle went into reserve, and the Hungarian 10th and 12th Infantry divisions were so weak they could only muster a small *kampfgruppe*.

The IX SS-Mountain Corps had a role to play in Operation *Konrad III*. Attacking from the Buda bridgehead to the south, they were to capture Budaörs Airport so that an air bridge could be re-established with a permanent airport. This would enable the evacuation of wounded troops, and would also provide an alternative to airdrops and gliders for delivering supplies. The axis of attack was along Budaörsi Road, and elements of Panzer Division Feldherrnhalle and 271st Volks-Grenadier Division, plus Hungarian assault artillery, were to join in.

The Soviets also regrouped some forces from Pest to Buda in order to reinforce the 2nd Ukrainian Front – not to take the Buda bridgehead, but to counter *Konrad III*. The units assigned comprised the 36th, 66th and 68th Guards Rifle divisions, and the 151st and 155th Rifle divisions. Also, the 59th Guards Rifle Division and the 113th Rifle Division, previously deployed in Buda, were withdrawn from the city and redeployed to counter *Konrad III*.

The task of eliminating the Buda bridgehead was now assigned to the Budapest Group, which moved its headquarters to southern Buda. Besides its own divisions – the 25th Guards Rifle Division and the 297th and 317th Rifle divisions – the Budapest Group also had control over the rest of the divisions remaining in Buda: the 108th and 109th Guards Rifle divisions, the 180th, 316th and 320th Rifle divisions and the 83rd Naval Infantry Brigade. In addition, it was also reinforced by two artillery divisions and two assault engineer brigades. The group had a total headcount of 43,000 troops but its fighting strength was below 25,000. More than 8,000 of the riflemen had submachine guns, and the attackers also had supporting armaments of *c.* 300 82mm and 100 120mm mortars, 100 45mm AT guns, 50 76mm mortars, and more than 50 howitzers. However, in terms of manpower, the Soviet numbers were far from superior, and their manpower supplies were dwindling. As a result, in the late-stage fighting, penal corps and then companies of Hungarian volunteers were also deployed, partly making good these shortcomings.

After the fall of Pest, however, Margit Island, located between the banks of the Danube, became the focus of military operations for a short time. On 19 January, the Soviets managed to transfer some AT artillery on the Danube to the bridgehead established the previous day on Margit Island. The German and Hungarian forces on the island noticed the Soviets crossing, but their attempt to eliminate the bridgehead came too late, and failed. The island was defended by parts of the Hungarian Academy Assault Battalion and the 22nd SS-Volunteer Cavalry Division.

In Buda, the Soviets managed to capture one of the key strongholds around Városmajor, then occupied half of the five-storey block on the corner of Szilágyi Erzsébet Alley off Trombitás Street. They then broke into the building of the Cogwheel Railway Station and charged the defenders in the defensive positions there, and captured Városmajor Park all the way to Szamos Street.

In the southern sector of the Buda bridgehead, the defenders repelled a minor Soviet attack on Sas Hill. Meanwhile, a company of the Vannay Battalion, sent to Farkasréti Cemetery as reinforcements, was

Emptied German parachute supply canisters. Even troops were forbidden from opening these containers: they had to be turned in, and the supplies were distributed from a central location. Yet, because the drops also included food supplies, both the civil population and soldiers regularly opened them on the spot. (Fortepan, 60138)

pinned down in the cemetery due to heavy fighting. A Soviet attack against the Lágymányos Railway Enbankment was also repelled.

Even after the fall of Pest, the German Budapest Supply Staff tried to supply the bridgehead via air transport. However, the approaches to Vérmező airfield had to be altered, and aircraft now reached the Danube south of Buda, before turning north to the Vérmező area. Control of this airfield became key.

Due to losses, the Budapest Supply Staff gradually decreased the number of daytime missions flown in favour of night flying. On 20 January, the Soviet troops that had crossed over to Margit Island failed to capture the defended buildings at its northern end. But on this day, the Danube froze over, and the 25th Guards Rifle Division managed to establish another bridgehead on the island around a 13th-century monastery.

On 21 January, the Soviets at the northern Margit Island bridgehead managed to capture one building serving as a German–Hungarian strongpoint, but a further strongpoint remained. Efforts were made to wipe out the other Soviet bridgehead to the south, but to no avail.

Major-General Ivan Afonin, commander of the Budapest Group, was wounded this day and Lieutenant-General Ivan Mefodyevich Managarov assumed command. Managarov planned to continue the elimination of the Buda bridgehead, crushing its northern sector. For this, however, Margit Island would have to be taken. In addition, on the Buda side, the central axis of attack would be in Városmajor Park close to Buda Castle. Managarov also wanted to neutralize the Schmidt Castle stronghold and the defences in Óbuda. He wanted to envelope and isolate the castle with one attack from Mátyás Hill, and another via Bécsi Road.

For the main attack in Városmajor Park, Managarov shortened the Soviet 108th Guards Rifle Division's front line, and reinforced the neighbouring 108th and 320th Rifle divisions by assigning an artillery brigade, an assault engineer battalion and a penal battalion. Manpower in the Soviet rifle divisions was low by this time: the 320th Rifle Division had fewer than 1,500 combatants. These two divisions were to advance in parallel and reach the Danube on the day the attack began, clearing the occupied terrain and splitting the bridgehead in two. Meanwhile, the Germans were deploying their forces earmarked for retaking Budaörs Airport, but the attack never took place.

Soviet 82mm mortars bombarding Budapest. (MTI Photo Archives, 753033)

In Városmajor Park, the Axis defenders did execute their planned counter-attack: the Vannay Battalion, with the support of two Hungarian Zrínyi assault guns and the German Europa Battalion, attacked to retake the previously lost strongpoints, and managed to repossess a small part of the park. The Hungarian forces recaptured the Cogwheel Railway terminal, in close combat, but it had been set ablaze during the fighting, and the ammunition and fuel stored there had exploded. The Germans, in parallel, managed to recapture the villa located at the present-day Körszálló Hotel and a few more houses on Bimbó Street. But the attackers suffered heavy losses in the fighting – the Vannay

Battalion lost 68 troops and the Germans 54 men.

On 22 January, Soviet troops managed to break the deadlock on Margit Island. The Soviet 25th Guards Rifle Division sent reinforcements to the bridgehead at the island monastery over the frozen Danube at night. In the morning, the forces at the bridgehead launched a successful attack and Soviet riflemen also managed to reach the Palatinus Baths on the other side of the island. With this, the island was now split in two, with the German defenders in the northern half of the island cut off from the Hungarians. Some of the surrounded troops successfully broke out during the night, but the rest remained. Soviet forces captured 300 prisoners on the island on this day. However, they did not manage to capture the Palatinus Baths building in the centre of the island from a resistance group of Hungarian university students located inside.

Soviet troops from the 3rd Ukrainian Front advance during street fighting in Budapest in January 1945. (Sovfoto/ Universal Images Group via Getty Images)

In Óbuda, an attack was launched near Bécsi Road to surround and overcome the Schmidt Castle defenders. The Soviet 109th Guards Rifle Division attacked southwards from Bécsi Road, sending all of its artillery units to the front line for support, and was also reinforced with an assault engineer battalion. The attack was successful, and the assault units reached the Roman amphitheatre, for the loss of 82 troops. The other axis of attack began from Zöldmál. Here, the Soviet 180th Rifle Division attacked towards Mátyás Hill, but the defenders, emplaced in the surrounding fortified buildings, repelled this.

In and around Várrosmajor Park, the Soviet 108th Guards Rifle Division and the 320th Rifle Division had launched the main thrust of the attack. However, despite all the reinforcements they had, the two divisions could not get past the stronghold of the Plant Protection Research Institute building, the Cog-wheel Railway Station, and the villa at the present-day Körszálló Hotel.

On 23 January, the situation on Margit Island again comprised a stand-off, with the Soviet 25th Guards Rifle Division unable to get past the Palatinus Baths, despite a 6,000-shells-per-hour preparatory artillery bombardment. The defenders still repelled two Soviet attacks, and even launched a counter-attack.

Meanwhile, in the northern part of the Buda bridgehead, in Óbuda, the Germans continued beating back the incursion of the Soviet 109th Guards Rifle Division, and launched two unsuccessful counter-attacks. The Soviet 180th Rifle Division, on the other hand, managed to reach Mátyás Hill, temporarily taking it before the defenders recaptured it the same day.

At Várrosmajor Park, the Soviet 108th Guards Rifle Division and the 320th Rifle Division renewed the previous day's assault. They still could not achieve a breakthrough, but managed to capture the Cog-wheel Railway Station and parts of Rókus Hill that had previously been no man's land.

On 24 January, on Margit Island, the Soviets were still unable to advance, with the Palatinus Baths defenders successfully repelling a company-size attack. To end the stand-off, the Soviet forces attempted another landing on the eastern shore of the island using a Soviet penal company. The island's defenders spotted the crossing forces and repelled them. The attackers were unable to establish another bridgehead, and lost 58 troops.

In Óbuda, the 109th Guards Rifle Division continued south and reached the Roman amphitheatre. The local German defenders, however, managed to block two Soviet incursions.

To ensure success in the main axis of attack in Városmajor Park, Managarov extended the breadth of the attack south of Városmajor and deployed the 316th Soviet Rifle Division there. He also deployed the regrouped Soviet 297th Rifle Division in Városmajor.

The 24 January attack by the Soviet 109th Guards Rifle Division and the 320th Rifle Division achieved neither a breakthrough nor any significant results. The attack of the 316th Soviet Rifle Division in Farkasréti Cemetery was also devoid of major achievements and the minimal progress was soon halted.

On 25 January, the situation on Margit Island remained unchanged, with the Soviet 25th Guards Rifle Division unable to advance, and the defenders repelling two attacks on the Palatinus Baths. Yet, the Soviets did manage to eliminate the remaining defenders surrounded at the northern tip of the island.

In Óbuda, the Soviet 109th Guards Rifle Division and the 320th Rifle Division were unable to make any significant progress, but the Soviet 297th Rifle Division arrived at Városmajor and switched to spearhead the attack, as it had done in the operations to eliminate the Pest bridgehead, in order to achieve a breakthrough. The division was therefore reinforced with two more artillery brigades, an engineer brigade, and two penal battalions. The 297th took over the 320th Rifle Division's front, south of the Cog-wheel Railway Station.

In Farkasréti Cemetery, a German–Hungarian counter-attack recaptured previously lost areas. The defenders of the cemetery now included 80 SS troops, a platoon of gendarmes and a platoon of the Vannay Battalion.

Along Bocskai Road, the Soviets increased their attacks. They surrounded the Army's Central Uniform Depot on Daróczi Street and its German defenders. A melee soon erupted in the factory, with Hungarian Zrínyi assault howitzers used, but the Germans trapped within could not be reached.

The newly deployed division's attack finally brought the results long-awaited by Managarov – it captured several strongholds and significant areas in the western half of Városmajor Park on this day. However, it lost 158 troops in the fighting. The Soviets also heavily attacked Kis-Sváb Hill, but the defenders managed to repel them for now. Here, the Vannay Battalion, reinforced with troops from the Hungarian 12th Reserve Division, even launched a counter-attack, though it was unsuccessful. At the bridgehead, Pfeffer-Wildenbruch was forced to use the reserves saved for the attack on Budaörs Airport to repel the intensifying Soviet attacks.

On 26 January, the situation on Margit Island remained unchanged. In Óbuda, the 109th Guards Rifle Division reached Zsigmond Square. The attacking forces in Városmajor were further reinforced with a mortar brigade regrouped from Pest, as well as additional penal battalions.

The attack of the Soviet 108th Guards Rifle Division, now reinforced with the penal battalions, was finally successful. The defences collapsed, and the Soviets captured several German strongholds in the eastern parts of Rókus Hill, and reached Vérhalom district.

In Városmajor, the 297th Rifle Division made further progress and captured Városmajor Park to the height of Csaba Street. The 300-strong Szabados Group, formed from the Hungarian 10th Infantry Division, was also deployed here but even this did not affect the status quo. The Soviets also managed to capture the southern slopes of Kis-Sváb Hill.

The Germans temporarily recaptured the Army's Central Uniform Depot on Daróczi Street with the support of Hungarian Zrínyi assault howitzers, and freed the troops trapped inside, yet, by the end of the day, the Soviets had the building permanently under control. The Budapest Group captured 25 blocks in Budapest on this day.

On 27 January, the situation on Margit Island remained unchanged. In the northern part of the Buda bridgehead, the Soviet 180th Rifle Division occupied Ferenc Hill and temporarily also Mátyás Hill, but the Germans recaptured the latter the same day. In Óbuda, the Soviet 109th Guards Rifle Division continued to the south and reached Bécsi Road.

As further reinforcements, two tank companies were reassigned to the divisions fighting in Városmajor, one to the Soviet 297th Rifle Division, the other to the 108th Guards Rifle Division. The Soviet 108th Guards Rifle Division successfully advanced towards the Danube, capturing the Baár-Madras Grammar School strongpoint and reaching Marczibányi Square. At the same time, the Soviet 297th Rifle Division reached Krisztina Boulevard at the corner of Vérmező. In parallel, the Soviet 320th Rifle Division routed the defenders still standing in Városmajor Street and in Városmajor from the direction of Kis-Sváb Hill, and secured full control over the latter.

The Germans launched an unsuccessful counter-attack against the Soviets from Vérmező. With this, they also reached Városmajor, but the Soviets countered the incursion by the end of the day. The Soviet 297th Rifle Division alone lost 93 troops on this day, but also captured 240 prisoners.

Once the Soviets reached the confines of Vérmező Park, the Germans moved subsequent airlandings further south, towards the central and southern areas of the airfield. However, although the presence of Soviet artillery greatly increased the risk to aircraft, planes continued to land. Operation *Konrad III* was aborted the same day, and with this, the chance of relieving Budapest evaporated, and the predicament of the defenders of the Buda bridgehead thus became critical.

On 28 January, the situation on Margit Island remained unchanged. In Óbuda, the Soviet 109th Guards Rifle Division captured the old cemetery at the foot of Mátyás Hill, to the rear of Schmidt Castle, threatening to undermine the latter's defence. The Germans gathered troops to recapture the cemetery but these were smashed by a Soviet artillery strike. They then attempted another counter-attack, but this too was repelled.

The advance of the Soviet 108th Guards Rifle Division again slowed down, and it captured only one part of Marczibányi Square. The attacking Soviet 297th Rifle Division also did not advance much towards Vérmező Park. The fighting was in the blocks between Vérmező and Városmajor, and the Soviet division lost 101 troops on this

German artillery prepares to defend against armoured attacks in Lövőház Street, Buda in January 1945. (ullstein bild via Getty Images)

THE BATTLE FOR BUDA, 18 JANUARY–10 FEBRUARY 1945

After taking Pest, the Soviets first occupied Margit Island, then, after reinforcing the Soviet forces in Buda, crushed the northern part of the bridgehead by the end of January 1945. The biggest battles were fought over the possession of Városmajor Park. After that, Soviet forces attacked the centre of the bridgehead, but advances were slow, and they gained ground only gradually. By the end of the siege, they focussed their attacks on Sas Hill and Gellért Hill in the southern part of the city, which they managed to take. The defenders were thus pushed back to Castle Hill and its vicinity.

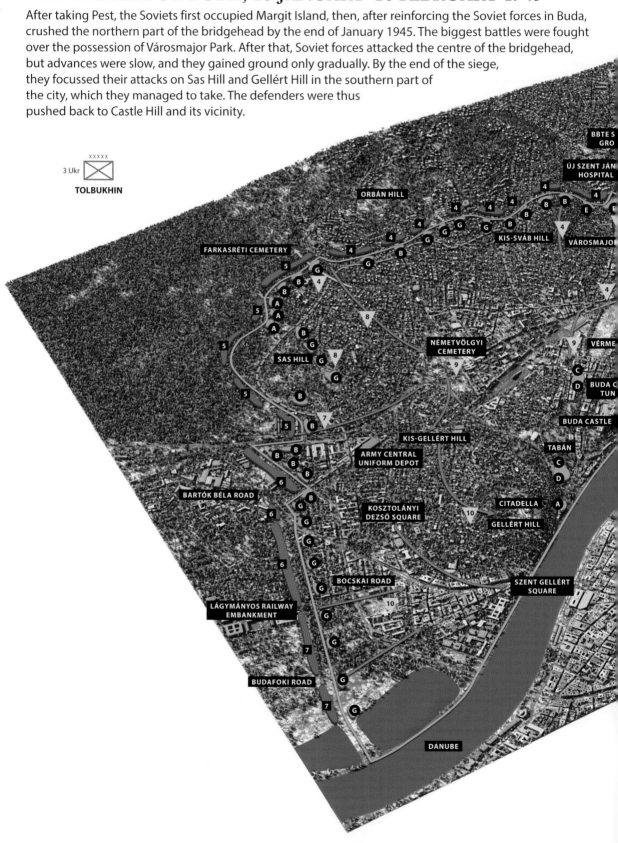

3 Ukr

TOLBUKHIN

BBTE S
GRO

ÚJ SZENT JÁN
HOSPITAL

ORBÁN HILL

KIS-SVÁB HILL

VÁROSMAJO

FARKASRÉTI CEMETERY

NÉMETVÖLGYI
CEMETERY

VÉRME

SAS HILL

BUDA C
TUN

BUDA CASTLE

KIS-GELLÉRT HILL

TABÁN

ARMY CENTRAL
UNIFORM DEPOT

CITADELLA

BARTÓK BÉLA ROAD

KOSZTOLÁNYI
DEZSŐ SQUARE

GELLÉRT HILL

BOCSKAI ROAD

SZENT GELLÉRT
SQUARE

LÁGYMÁNYOS RAILWAY
EMBANKMENT

BUDAFOKI ROAD

DANUBE

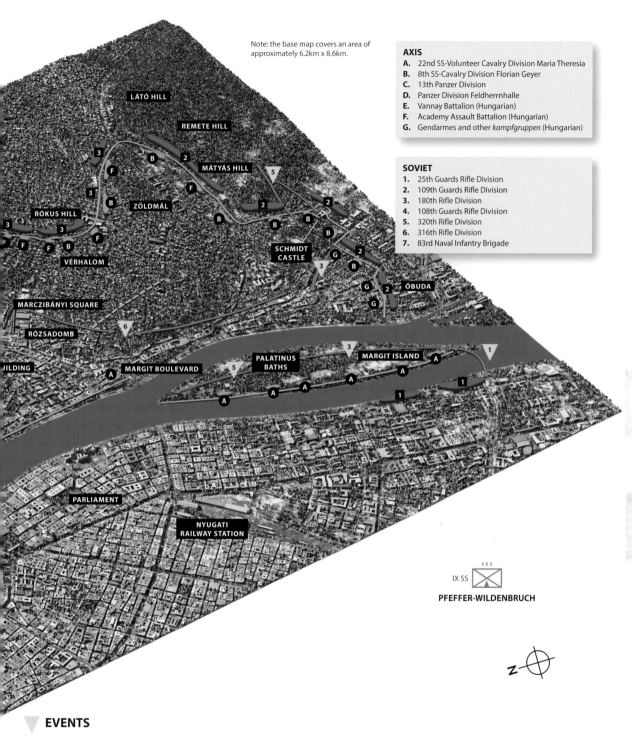

Note: the base map covers an area of approximately 6.2km x 8.6km.

AXIS

A. 22nd SS-Volunteer Cavalry Division Maria Theresia
B. 8th SS-Cavalry Division Florian Geyer
C. 13th Panzer Division
D. Panzer Division Feldherrnhalle
E. Vannay Battalion (Hungarian)
F. Academy Assault Battalion (Hungarian)
G. Gendarmes and other *kampfgruppen* (Hungarian)

SOVIET

1. 25th Guards Rifle Division
2. 109th Guards Rifle Division
3. 180th Rifle Division
4. 108th Guards Rifle Division
5. 320th Rifle Division
6. 316th Rifle Division
7. 83rd Naval Infantry Brigade

LÁTÓ HILL

REMETE HILL

MÁTYÁS HILL

ZÖLDMÁL

RÓKUS HILL

VÉRHALOM

SCHMIDT CASTLE

ÓBUDA

MARCZIBÁNYI SQUARE

RÓZSADOMB

BUILDING

MARGIT BOULEVARD

PALATINUS BATHS

MARGIT ISLAND

PARLIAMENT

NYUGATI RAILWAY STATION

IX SS

PFEFFER-WILDENBRUCH

EVENTS

1. 19 January 1945: The Soviet 25th Guards Rifle Division crosses over from Pest and establishes a bridgehead on Margit Island. In Buda, the 108th Guards Division breaks through the defences of the Vannay Battalion in Városmajor and manages to advance to Temes Street.

2. 22 January 1945: The Vannay Battalion launches a successful counter-attack in Városmajor.

3. 22 January 1945: Soviet forces manage to break out of the two bridgeheads on Margit Island and occupy the northern part of the island up to the Palatinus Baths. The 109th Soviet Rifle Division manages to advance to the Roman Amphitheatre along Bécsi Road.

4. 25–26 January 1945: Soviet forces occupy Városmajor up to Csaba Street. Also, several strongholds around Városmajor (including the villa on the site of Körszálló Hotel, and the Baár-Madras Grammar School) fall, with Kis-Sváb Hill following the next day.

5. 29 January 1945: The Soviets occupy the rest of Margit Island, as well as Schmidt Castle and Mátyás Hill in Buda, thus causing the collapse of the northern section of the Buda defences.

6. 30 January 1945: German and Hungarian forces withdraw from the northern part of the bridgehead, retreating to Margit Boulevard.

7. 1 February 1945: The Soviets launch their assault along Budaörsi Road.

8. 3–4 February 1945: Soviet troops take Farkasréti Cemetery and Sas Hill, and also advance to Németvölgyi Cemetery.

9. 9 February 1945: Soviet forces attack towards the Buda Castle Tunnel, and occupy Kis-Gellért Hill in southern Buda.

10. 10 February 1945: The Soviets break through the defences of the Lágymányos Railway Embankment. With this, southern Buda falls, with the exception of the Citadella, which is secured the following day.

A Carro Armato M15/42 tank of the German 12th SS-Police Panzer Company on the corner of Nagyszombat and Lajos streets in the Óbuda district of Budapest. (MTI Photo Archives, 753127)

The Royal Palace (now known as Buda Castle) burning. The palace was set on fire several times during the siege, and some parts of it were completely burnt out. (Fortepan, 175146)

day. The defending German troops on the edge of Vérmező tried to oust the attackers with several counter-attacks, all of which were unsuccessful. Pfeffer-Wildenbruch deployed parts of the German 13th Panzer Division to reinforce the defences here. On the 28th, the Soviet 316th Rifle Division was the most successful among the attacking forces, capturing Orbán Hill. The Soviet 320th Rifle Division continued to advance towards Déli Railway Station, repelling two counter-attacks as it progressed.

On 29 January, the situation on Margit Island finally changed. The artillery previously providing fire support to the defenders on the Buda side from Óbuda was now threatened by the Soviet advances, and could no longer do so. The Soviet 25th Guards Rifle Division's attack against the Palatinus Baths finally succeeded. The remaining defenders retreated to the south to the Casino building, the last line of defence on the island. However, the bridgehead was already so narrow that the defenders' mortar fire was falling back on their own positions. Yet, the defenders still held the southern point of the island. In the evening, however, the rest of the island was evacuated, and the still-standing section of Margit Bridge, towards Buda, was demolished.

The Soviet 180th Rifle Division finally captured Mátyás Hill, and the buildings on Bécsi Road near Schmidt Castle were also taken by the 109th Rifle Division. The castle thus became completely cut off. One of the penal companies moved in to attack the castle, and all its defenders were killed or captured. With this, the German defences in the Óbuda district collapsed. The Soviet 109th Guards Rifle Division lost 54 troops on this day, and captured 180 prisoners.

The Soviet 108th Guards Rifle Division could not get past Vérhalom Square, but managed to capture all of Marczibányi Square. The Soviet 297th Rifle Division took several blocks on the corner of Vérmező, and the fight for capturing the Post Building began. The Soviet forces that passed through Attila Road, however, were neutralized by the defenders. The 297th Rifle Division lost 135 troops over the course of the day.

The Soviet 320th and 316th Rifle divisions could still only advance slowly towards Déli Railway Station. The 317th Rifle Division arrived in the southern Buda sector to replace the 316th Rifle Division, and attacked towards the north of Sas Hill.

Fearing that his troops in the northern part of the bridgehead would be surrounded, Pfeffer-Wildenbruch withdrew his remaining forces to Margit Boulevard, evacuating Rózsadomb Hill.

On 30 January, the Soviet forces following the German and Hungarian troops evacuating Rózsadomb Hill captured many prisoners and much materiel. The 108th Guards Rifle Division finally managed to reach the Danube, and surrounded a large group of cut-off defenders on Szemlő Hill, capturing 2,500 of them. However, their attack stalled at Margit Boulevard.

The fight for Széll Kálmán Square also began this day. The 297th Soviet Rifle Division captured the Post Building and the Attila Road School on the edge of Vérmező Park – the latter formed a strongpoint defended by the Hungarian Budapest Guard Battalion. Soviet troops occupied a building on the corner of Bors Street and Vérmező Park, but Hungarian gendarmes attacked and set the building on fire, displacing them. Soviet forces attacked the Post Building, supported by flame-throwers, which ignited coal piled up in the courtyard and set the building on fire. Yet, the Vannay Battalion troops defending it remained, retreating to the top floor using the snow there to keep cool.

The Soviet 320th Rifle Division continued to slowly advance towards Déli Railway Station. The 316th and 317th Rifle divisions also attacked but to minimal effect. Yet another attack on the eastern section of the Lágymányos Railway Embankment failed to achieve anything, as the Hungarian Viharos Battle Group had been reinforced with a company on this day.

To crush the northern part of the Buda bridgehead, Managarov's plan was for the 299th Rifle Division to attack from the north, and the 317th Rifle Division from the south, to break through the lines between Kis-Sváb and Sas hills, then surround and destroy the defences, thereby eliminating the Buda bridgehead's central sector.

On 31 January, the Soviets captured the Attila Road School and the entire block, and reached Mátray and Logodi streets, at the threshold of Buda Castle. In Farkasréti Cemetery, the strength of the SS company was now down to 18 troops, yet they managed to recover two lost strongholds on Mártonhegyi and Bürök roads with the support of Hungarian Zrínyi assault howitzers. Construction began on the defences of Castle Hill on this day – comprising a triple-layered system of strongpoints. The streets were blocked by barricades and tank ditches. The Budapest Group captured 12 blocks in Budapest on the 31st.

A Soviet assault group attacking a factory in Buda in February 1945. (MTI Photo Archives, 753146)

In the course of January 1945, the IX SS-Mountain Corps lost 27,500 troops, of which 4,500 were killed, 21,000 injured and 2,000 missing.

On 1 February, the defenders of the Post Building received reinforcements. The Germans also launched an unsuccessful counter-attack from the direction of Orbán Hill towards Kis-Sváb Hill. Meanwhile, the focus of military operations shifted to southern Buda where the Soviet forces attacked to the north along Budaörsi Road, next to Sas Hill, with the support of T-34 tanks, resulting in a penetration in depth. The Soviet forces also continued to slowly advance towards Déli Railway Station in the central sector. The Budapest Group took 130 blocks in Budapest this day.

FIGHTING AT THE VÉRMEZŐ SCHOOL, BUDA, 0800HRS, 31 JANUARY 1945 (PP.76–77)

The Vérmező Park airfield in Buda played a key role in the course of the siege of Budapest. Following the fall of the permanent airports and the Pest bridgehead, the Vérmező Park was the only suitable terrain on which aircraft could land. From the outset of the siege, the airfield was used by courier planes for take-off and landing, then, from 1 January 1945, German cargo gliders started to use the field to bring in supplies. The wreckage of these planes can be seen in several period photographs. The airfield was also used to drop parachute containers. Thus, keeping hold of Vérmező was of strategic importance to maintain the Axis supply chains.

With the fall of nearby Kis-Sváb Hill, Soviet forces secured the necessary vantage point to bombard the park with artillery, and Soviet troops also began to infiltrate parts of the airfield. They first reached the buildings on Krisztina Boulevard. They then moved on to take Vérmező by first trying to occupy a school building (1) located at the northern edge of the park. The defenders withdrew and reformed their defensive line among the houses on the eastern edge of Vérmező. The school building was defended by Hungarian troops (2), and also had a dressing station in the basement. A long and bloody struggle ensued for control of the school building (shown here, with Soviet troops in the attack, (3) and it changed hands several times in the weeks that followed. During the siege, an AT trench (4) was dug in front of the school building, and in some sections tanks that had been captured by Axis forces in 1941 (5) were used to bolster the defence.

On 2 February, the Post Building had 37 defenders, and in the buildings to the west of Vérmező Park, 59 troops with nine machine guns were emplaced. The Hungarians recaptured the Attila Road School. The Soviets pulled back from the Post Building. In addition, a group of Hungarian volunteers managed to cross Széll Kálmán Square and destroyed the Soviet battalion command headquartered in Városmajor Street School. Hoping to break through in the central bridgehead sector, the Soviet 297th Rifle Division's section of front line north of Géli Railway Station was taken over by the 180th Rifle Division. The 297th was thus able to concentrate its strength in the attack, and the 316th and 320th Rifle divisions also joined in on its flank. However, despite all this, the Soviets did not break through or advance significantly, but they did successfully repel several German tank-supported counter-attacks. The Budapest Group lost 419 troops on this day and took 573 prisoners.

On 3 February, the Soviets deployed a company of Hungarian volunteer soldiers, who had surrendered to them, against the Axis defenders in Vérmező. Soviet forces surrounded the Germans and Hungarians in Farkasréti Cemetery. The Soviets also began a battle for Sas Hill but achieved only modest results. The defenders also repelled the Soviets' tank-supported attacks along Budaörsi and Bocskai roads, destroying three tanks, two of which using panzerfausts.

On 4 February, German and Hungarian forces repelled a tank-supported Soviet attack from the direction of Városmajor Park and Széll Kálmán Square. The Soviet advance near Déli Railway Station still remained slow. In Farkasréti Cemetery, the Soviets neutralized the defenders surrounded the day before. The Soviet 25th Guards Rifle Division's attack from Nématvölgyi Cemetery, however, was unsuccessful – the Hungarian artillery troops surrendered, but the Germans still held the cemetery.

Mangarov's attacks over the previous days in the central sector had yielded modest results, so he shifted the focus of attack to the southern section of the bridgehead. This involved getting his troops out to the Danube in the Tabán district, thereby isolating the defenders of Gellért Hill and its surroundings to the south, who could then be neutralized. For this, the Soviet troops first had to secure Sas Hill, a task assigned to the 316th and 317th Rifle divisions. On their flank, to the north, was the 25th Guards Rifle Division, transferred from Margit Island. The Soviet plan was to surround the defenders of Sas Hill.

On 5 February, the Post Building was abandoned by the defenders because it was now within range of Soviet artillery in Vérmező Park. The siege of Déli Railway Station began. The Germans reinforced this central sector – creating barricades from rail wagons, for instance. The defenders repelled the Soviet attack on Sas Hill, but at the same time, another Soviet attack started from Budaörsi Road, reaching the BAH Junction. Nématvölgyi Cemetery also fell. The Soviets also deployed vehicles equipped with flame-throwers in the fighting. On Karolina Road, a Hungarian counter-attack was repelled. Yet another Soviet attack on the eastern section of the Lágymányos Railway Embankment still achieved nothing.

On 6 February, the Soviet 316th and 317th divisions, supported by tanks, captured Sas Hill in close combat. The remaining defenders there tried to break out towards Buda Castle. The 320th Rifle Division broke into the western part of Nématvölgyi Cemetery. With the fall of Sas Hill, another key point in the defence was lost; moreover, Soviet artillery units now deployed to the hill. The Soviet 297th Rifle Division captured No. 11 Honvéd Hospital this day and reached Alkotás Road near Déli Railway Station. During the day, Soviet forces captured 2,700 prisoners of war (including hundreds of wounded troops from the military hospitals).

In and around Buda Castle, the defenders now had 11,000 wounded troops – food was scarce and they were each given only 15 grams of legumes and half a slice of bread a day. The Budapest Group captured 16 blocks in Budapest on this day.

On 7 February, a Soviet assault group broke into a building on Várfok Street, but a Hungarian counter-attack repelled the Soviet incursion. Fighting erupted around Déli Railway Station. The Germans launched a counter-attack to take back the station, managing to recapture the western half. Of the defenders who broke out from Sas Hill the day before, a company-sized group of Germans reached Buda Castle. The Soviets captured Németvölgyi Cemetery. The Budapest Group lost 333 troops on the 7th.

On 8 February, German defenders trapped on the upper story of a building on Krisztina Boulevard, on the edge of Vérmező, were rescued by a Hungarian group transiting Vérmező Park; those Germans who could walk then returned to Attila Road. The Germans withdrew their defences to the eastern perimeter of Vérmező Park. The Soviet 297th Rifle Division continued the fight to capture Déli Railway Station and its surroundings.

The focus of Soviet attacks remained southern Buda, however. The Soviet 317th Rifle Division, supported by tanks, cleared the area to the fore of Sas Hill, then the 317th and the 320th Rifle divisions infiltrated the western part of Gellért Hill, repelling two German counter-attacks on the go. The Budapest Group lost 381 troops on this day.

On 9 February, a 20-strong Soviet assault group recaptured the Attila Road School at Vérmező, then made for Buda Castle, but German and Hungarian troops recaptured the building, and destroyed the Soviet group with panzerfausts; only three of them survived. Soviet forces secured Déli Railway Station, then moved on towards the Buda Castle Tunnel. In southern Buda, the 25th Guards Rifle Division in Németvölgyi Cemetery continued eastwards in the Tabán district. The Soviet 320th Rifle Division captured Kis-Gellért Hill and the artillery positions there were taken in hand to hand fighting.

A Hungarian armoured train near Gellért Hill during the siege of Budapest. (Süddeutsche Zeitung/Alamy)

A battle erupted for the western parts of Gellért Hill. Also, south of Gellért Hill, the Soviets reached what is today Kosztolányi Dezső Square, and a fight broke out for control of it. The Soviets repelled several tank-supported German counter-attacks on this day. The Soviets launched another unsuccessful attack on the eastern section of the Lágymányos Railway Embankment. The Budapest Group lost 342 troops, and captured 10 blocks on the 9th.

On 10 February, the Soviets retook the Attila Road School, and they also deployed a company of Hungarian volunteers. The Soviet 297th Rifle

Division mopped up at Déli Railway Station. The Soviet 108th Guards Rifle Division advanced to Krisztina Square, approaching the Buda Castle Tunnel. The Soviets thus reached the Buda Castle perimeter both at the edge of Vérmező Park and at Krisztina Square, while the 317th Rifle Division made it to Gellért Hill. In southern Buda, the Soviet 25th Guards Rifle Division in Németvölgyi Cemetery entered Tabán, and threatened to cut off the defenders to the south by striking at the Danube. The Soviet 320th Rifle Division captured the western half of Gellért Hill where the defenders resolutely tried to hold all the buildings. South of Gellért Hill, the Soviets captured modern Kosztolányi Dezső Square, Bartók Béla Road and Szent Gellért Square. Parts of the Hungarian 10th Infantry Division surrendered on Bartók Béla Road. The Viharos Battle Group abandoned the eastern sector of the Lágymányos Railway Embankment and retreated, then surrendered south of Gellért Hill. The whole of southern Buda fell on this day with the exception of the Citadella, which the Soviets captured on the 11th. The Budapest Group lost 385 troops, and captured 15 blocks on this day.

German prisoners of war in Móricz Zsigmond Square, in Buda. (MTI Photo Archives, FMAFI1945_28034)

BREAKOUT: 11–13 FEBRUARY 1945

Although Hitler had declared Budapest a fortress and forbidden any breakouts, the latter had already been considered at the outset of the siege, when Iván Hindy raised the idea (subsequently rejected) at the end of December 1944. However, even the German commanders considered the no-breakout order as non-binding. During the relief attempts, on 6 January, Pfeffer-Windenbruch had already asked his high command in which direction he should prepare to break out to link up with the approaching relief units. The high command gave Budaörs or the Pilis Mountains as two possibilities. On 8 January, the IX SS-Mountain Corps planned to break out towards the Pilis Mountains, but Hitler ordered Army Group South to forbid it. After Operation *Konrad III* was aborted, a breakout was once again discussed, but Pfeffer-Windenbruch rejected this.

At the beginning of February, the continual shrinking of the Buda bridgehead made clear it could not be held for long. Soviet forces were already directly threatening Castle Hill from Széll Kálmán and Krisztina squares. By 11 February, the defenders had only a day's supply of ammunition left, minimal numbers of artillery shells, and heavily depleted food reserves. The defenders would have lasted only a day or two at most. Despite Hitler's orders to the contrary, Pfeffer-Windenbruch now reconsidered the breakout question.

Before the breakout, Axis strength stood at 24,000 German and 20,000 Hungarian troops. However, this number also included 9,600 German and 2,000 Hungarian injured soldiers. Thus, attempting to break out, instead of surrendering, was not a surprising choice; indeed, some troops would indeed

Abandoned infantry fighting vehicles of the 13th Panzer Division in Fő Street in the wake of the Axis breakout. (Fortepan, 31801)

reach friendly positions after doing so. The breakout involved 16,000 troops, less than half the number of defenders – most were Germans, whereas the Hungarians generally chose not to, even those who initially were keen to do so.

Based on post-war data, it is now known that only a very small percentage of German troops captured in Budapest later returned to Germany from captivity. Of course, many Hungarians also died in captivity, but not nearly as many as the Germans. Also, it was easier for Hungarian troops to blend in as civilians in non-uniform, and speaking Hungarian, thus avoiding captivity. Some SS troops, recruited in Hungary, did manage to do this too.

Another factor to be considered for the Germans is that the forces fighting in Budapest included two SS-cavalry divisions. The Soviets were unforgiving towards surrendering SS soldiers. Many were executed after capture, with the Eastern auxiliary troops fighting alongside the Germans sharing this same fate, without even reaching the prison camps. The Soviets had already executed prisoners after crushing the Pest bridgehead, and there were similar incidents on the Buda side prior to the breakout. All things considered, the Germans were more inclined to attempt to break out, whereas the Hungarians were more likely to remain and surrender.

Pfeffer-Wildenbruch finally ordered the breakout on 11 February, but now there was not enough time to make the necessary preparations. He telegrammed the order to Berlin that afternoon, then destroyed the radio so that Hitler could not veto by reply. He briefed the German staff first, and then the Hungarian staff after them. The troops were briefed only a few hours before the actual breakout. They were thus able to keep the plan a secret, but preparations were poor.

The Soviets were aware that a breakout attempt was to be expected. They were familiar with German military procedures. Further, captured Hungarian troops also gave away information on the expected German breakout, rumours of which had been circulating for weeks. The precise time and location remained unclear. Yet, due to the geography of Buda, a westward breakout seemed the most likely.

Pfeffer-Wildenbruch's decision to keep the plans a secret had its merits, yet, it did not leave enough time to arrange proper support for the breakout. The defenders also had to destroy all munitions and supplies they could not take with them, including a large number of tanks on Nap Hill and around Castle Hill. The injured also could not be transported. Those with light wounds could join in the breakout, but the rest were left in the emergency hospitals below Buda Castle.

For those who would join the breakout attempt, Bécsi kapu Square in Buda Castle and nearby Mária Square were designated as gathering points. The breakout was planned to happen in two directions through Széna Square and Margit Boulevard. According to German intel, the Soviet defences were weaker there, but this was a misassumption. After breaking through the Soviet blockade, the troops were to move westwards. The forests around Nagykovácsi were designated a rendezvous point. From there, depending on the situation, they would move on towards Szomor and Máriahalom to join friendly forces, or, if this was impossible, they would reroute via the Pilis Hills. The breakout forces also requested support from German fighters and the bombing of the Soviet reserves to facilitate the breakout.

The breakout forces were divided into three waves. The first was to break through the Soviet blockade. This wave was mainly made up of German troops, and only a few Hungarians were assigned to it, including the Vannay Battalion, and some Hungarians with local knowledge of the Buda Hills who were to help the groups that escaped in navigating. Most Hungarians who joined the breakout attempt were assigned to the second wave, as were the rest of the German units. The third wave comprised only the rearguard and the injured. The breakout also had armour support of a total of five tanks and a few assault guns. Pfeffer-Wildenbruch and the staff of the IX SS-Mountain Corps, as well as Iván Hindy and the staff of the Hungarian First Corps, however, did not join the troops above ground but set off with a 500-strong *kampfgruppe* using the underground bed of Ördög-árok Canal to bypass the Soviet positions, aiming to link up with the breakout forces at Hűvösvölgyi Road.

The first wave set off on 11 February at 2000hrs through Széna Square. Tanks and armoured guns spearheaded the attack, and the first group, though suffering heavy losses, did break through the positions of the Soviet 180th Rifle Division. However, some of the Soviet forces retreated into the surrounding buildings, and continued to oppose the breakout. On the Soviet side, the situation was so severe that even supply corps troops had to take up arms. The attack on Margit Boulevard, on the other hand, was unsuccessful and was pinned down by Soviet artillery fire from the outset. The breakout suffered the greatest losses here, with at least 600 troops killed on Margit Boulevard and in Széna Square.

For those who made it out of Széna Square, the attack continued along two axes: one branched along modern Szilágyi Erzsébet Alley and Városmajor Street in the direction of Hűvösvölgy district, and the other detoured to the north towards Rózsadomb Hill, but also in the general direction of Hűvösvölgy. The first wave continued westwards, but the Soviet 337th Rifle Division, arriving from Hűvösvölgy this same day, halted them on 12 February around Bólyai Academy. The command staff, who had transited Ördög-árok Canal and were now above ground, were also halted. Groups from the first wave tried to proceed at a tangent, but they became isolated over time. The first wave was thus surrounded, but the troops still defended in the various blocks for days before surrendering or being neutralized. Pfeffer-Wildenbruch surrendered in a building near Bólyai Academy. Iván Hindy and his staff

Exhausted German troops, having survived the breakout from Budapest, rest on a German AFV. (ullstein bild via Getty Images)

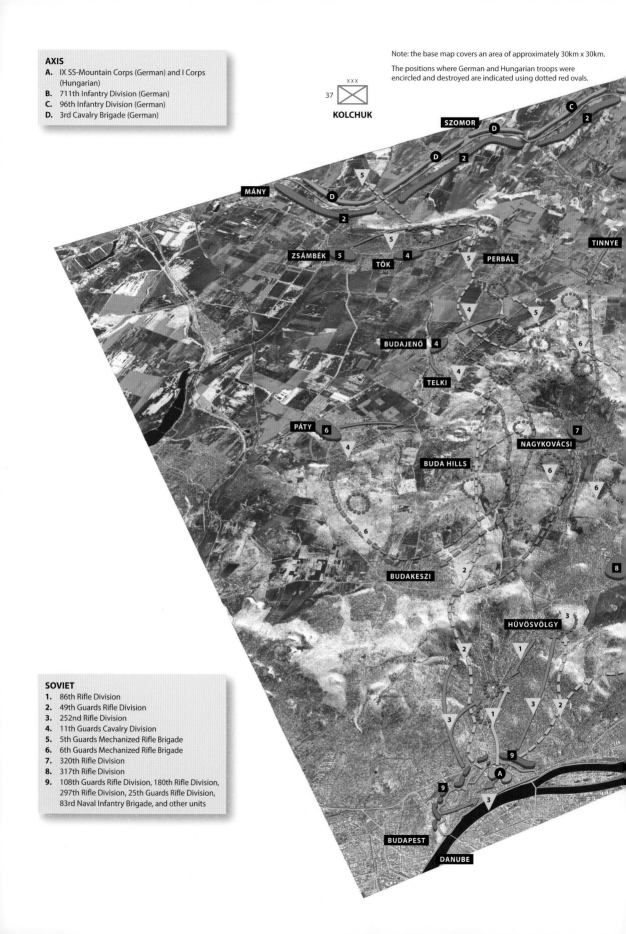

AXIS

A. IX SS-Mountain Corps (German) and I Corps (Hungarian)
B. 711th Infantry Division (German)
C. 96th Infantry Division (German)
D. 3rd Cavalry Brigade (German)

Note: the base map covers an area of approximately 30km x 30km.

The positions where German and Hungarian troops were encircled and destroyed are indicated using dotted red ovals.

37 ⊠ xxx

KOLCHUK

SZOMOR
MÁNY
ZSÁMBÉK
TÖK
PERBÁL
TINNYE
BUDAJENŐ
TELKI
PÁTY
NAGYKOVÁCSI
BUDA HILLS
BUDAKESZI
HÜVÖSVÖLGY
BUDAPEST
DANUBE

SOVIET

1. 86th Rifle Division
2. 49th Guards Rifle Division
3. 252nd Rifle Division
4. 11th Guards Cavalry Division
5. 5th Guards Mechanized Rifle Brigade
6. 6th Guards Mechanized Rifle Brigade
7. 320th Rifle Division
8. 317th Rifle Division
9. 108th Guards Rifle Division, 180th Rifle Division, 297th Rifle Division, 25th Guards Rifle Division, 83rd Naval Infantry Brigade, and other units

THE BUDA MOUNTAINS, 11–16 FEBRUARY 1945

The first wave of the Axis breakout, starting from Bécsi kapu Square in Buda Castle and nearby Mária Square, broke through the Soviet blockade, but did not manage to pass through Hűvösvölgy and reach the rallying point in the forests around Nagykovácsi. The next breakout waves, however, did manage to reach the rallying point from the flanks through the wooded hills. But the Soviets had established a blockade around the woods, and only a few of the troops that emerged from the trees to the west of Nagykovácsi managed to make it through the Soviet blockade and reach friendly lines.

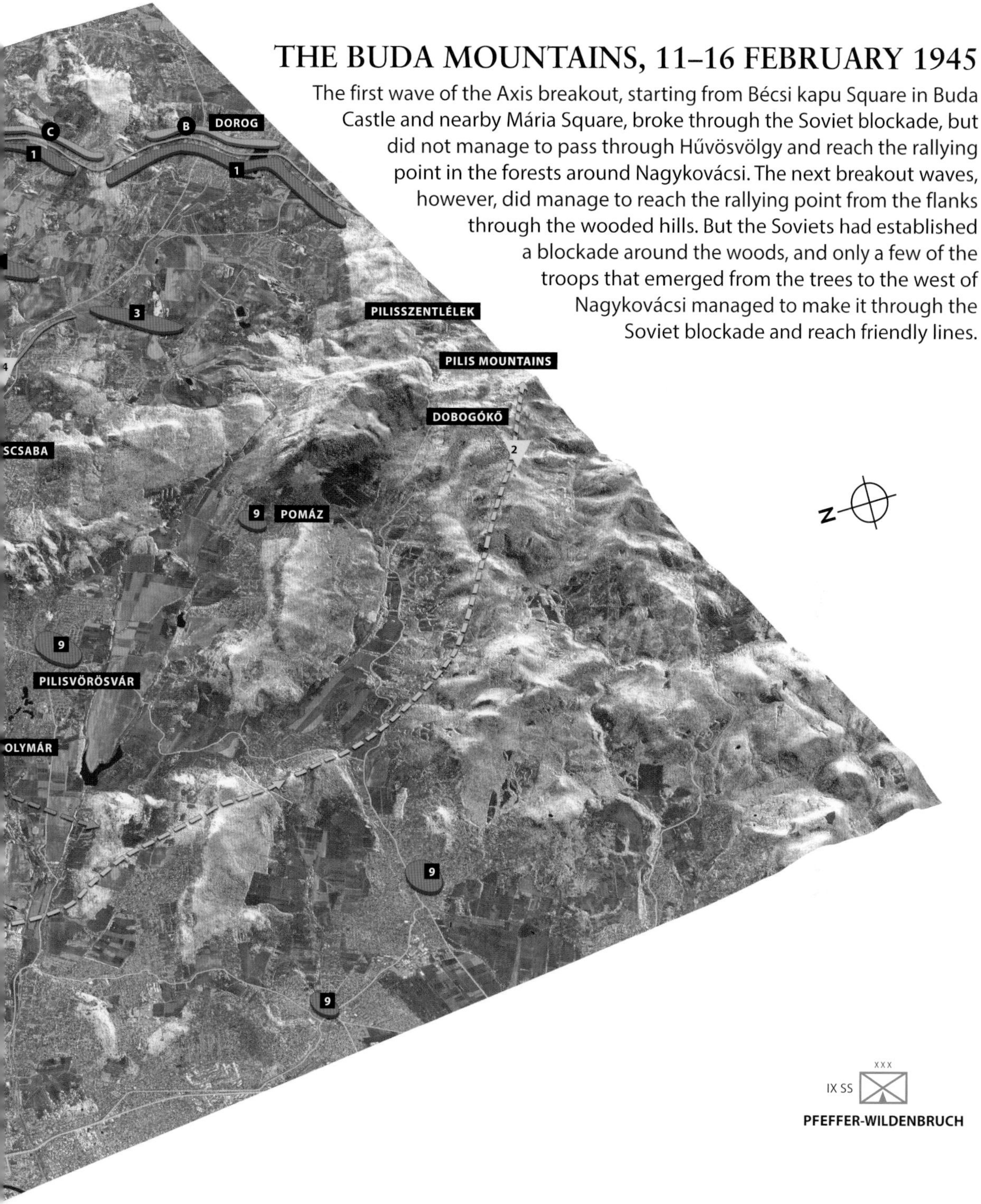

C
1
B **DOROG**
1
3
4
PILISSZENTLÉLEK
PILIS MOUNTAINS
DOBOGÓKŐ
SCSABA
2
9 **POMÁZ**
9
PILISVÖRÖSVÁR
OLYMÁR
9
9

IX SS
PFEFFER-WILDENBRUCH

EVENTS

1. 11 February 1945: The first wave of the breakout makes it through the defences of the Soviet 180th Rifle Division and advances to Bólyai Academy along Szilágyi Erzsébet Alley, where further progress is blocked by the Soviet 337th Rifle Division.

2. Further waves of German and Hungarian breakout troops pass through the breached lines of the 180th Rifle Division and leave Budapest, heading towards Hármashatár Hill and Budakeszi. They reach the rallying point in the forests around Nagykovácsi through the wooded hilly area.

3. 12–13 February 1945: Soviet troops capture Castle Hill without encountering any significant resistance, and move forward to pursue the troops breaking out from Buda.

4. The Soviet 11th Cavalry Division, the 19th Rifle Division and the 49th Guards Rifle Division establish a blockade on the line Piliscsaba–Tinnye–Perbál–Budajenő–Telki–Páty around the forests surrounding Nagykovácsi.

5. 14 February 1945 onwards: The breakout troops begin their attempts en masse to reach friendly positions passing through the Nagykovácsi forests towards the west. The Soviets capture and eliminate most groups emerging from the forest, but a few hundred troops still manage to reach friendly positions.

6. 13–16 February 1945: The Soviet blockading forces begin to comb through the forests, eliminating all breakout troops still sheltering there.

ASSAULT ON THE CITADELLA FORT, BUDA, 0800HRS, 12 FEBRUARY 1945 (PP. 86–87)

The Citadella fort (**1**), built in the 19th century, regained military importance during World War II. The Hungarian air defence command for southern Buda was headquartered here, and the fort was also equipped with air-defence searchlights. With the capital surrounded, German forces also concentrated here. During the siege, the fort was regularly attacked by the Soviet Air Forces (**2**), but they could not break down its thick walls.

By the evening of 11 February 1945, the Soviets had captured most of Gellért Hill, but not the Citadella. By this time, only a German–Hungarian rearguard still held the fort. The next morning, troops of the Soviet 83rd Naval Infantry Brigade (**3**) and the 316th Rifle Division, supported by T-34 tanks (**4**), approached the fort from the south, and managed to break in and capture it in close combat. Afterwards, the Soviets used the fort to hold Axis prisoners of war.

turned back, and were captured on Krisztina Boulevard. Three divisional commanders fell in surface battles in the first breakout wave: Gerhard Schmidhuber, August Zehender and Joachim Rumohr.

The second and third waves of the breakout were more fortunate. The first wave had pierced the blockade. The Soviet groups still fighting around Széna Square were either eliminated by the second wave, or some of them withdrew. Thus, from late in the evening on 11 February until around 0600hrs on 12 February, the breakout units were able to move from Castle Hill to Rózsadomb Hill without significant resistance. Several thousand troops broke out this way, heading for Nagykovácsi via Hármashatár Hill. Another large group from Panzer Division Feldherrnhalle were lucky to pass through Vérmező Park between the positions of the 180th and 297th Rifle divisions without fighting, and then headed for Budakeszi. This group also consisted of several thousand troops.

On 12 and 13 February, the breakout forces, around 8,000 strong, reached the forests around Nagykovácsi. However, by this time, the Soviet 11th Cavalry Division, the 19th Rifle Division and the 49th Guards Rifle Division had established a blockade along the Piliscsaba–Tinnye–Perbál–Budajenő–Telki–Páty line to the west and north of the forests around Nagykovácsi. The Soviet 2nd Guards Mechanized Corps was also in this area.

In the morning of 12 February, the Soviet 180th Division around Széna Square restored the blockade. The Soviet 25th Guards Rifle Division successfully invaded Tabán and reached the Danube, and by dawn, the clearing of the Citadella was also completed. The 297th Rifle Division and, from the south, the 83rd Naval Infantry Brigade attacked Castle Hill, with no significant resistance to deter their advances. On 13 February, the whole of the Buda bridgehead fell to the Soviets, with only a few surrounded breakout groups still resisting in Buda, such as in the Új Szent János Hospital.

From 14 February, the breakout forces in the Nagykovácsi woods launched attempts to reach friendly forces to the west. Few among them chose to take the longer route through the Pilis Mountains: most went west (towards Perbál and Telki). However, the Soviets were waiting on the other side for those exiting the forest. Nevertheless, several hundred managed to get through, with the largest group numbering around 300 troops. On 12 and 13 February, 27 troops made it through, 650 on 14 February, and 108 thereafter, for a total of 785 troops. Eighty of these were Hungarians, and the rest were Germans. All the other troops who had broken out were either killed, captured or executed after surrendering. They were buried in unmarked mass graves in the Buda Hills, which remain unexhumed today. The siege of Budapest was over.

Hungarian military prisoners of war on Nagykörút Boulevard; note the cobblestone barricade in the background. (MTI Photo Archives, 753035)

Eastern Europe, 15 October 1944–15 February 1945

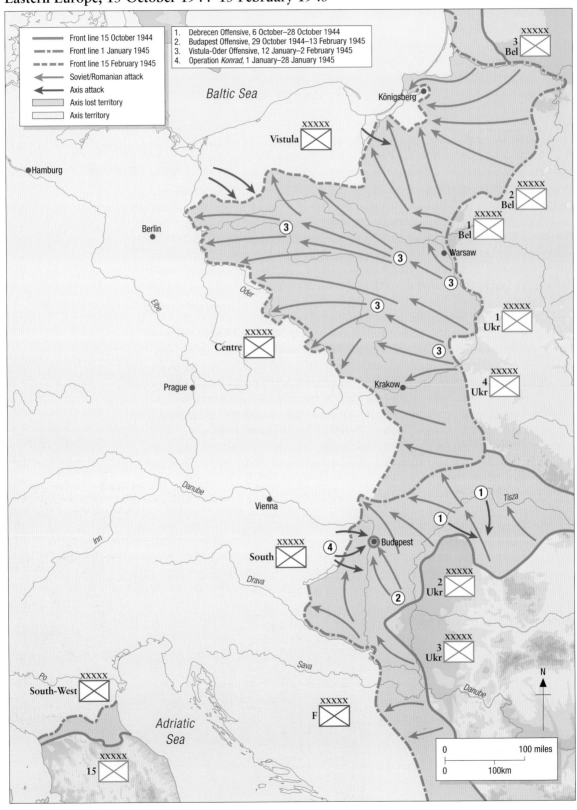

Front line 15 October 1944
Front line 1 January 1945
Front line 15 February 1945
Soviet/Romanian attack
Axis attack
Axis lost territory
Axis territory

1. Debrecen Offensive, 6 October–28 October 1944
2. Budapest Offensive, 29 October 1944–13 February 1945
3. Vistula-Oder Offensive, 12 January–2 February 1945
4. Operation *Konrad*, 1 January–28 January 1945

Baltic Sea

Königsberg

Vistula

Hamburg

Berlin

Elbe

Oder

Warsaw

3 Bel

2 Bel

1 Bel

1 Ukr

Centre

Prague

Krakow

4 Ukr

Danube

Vienna

Inn

South

Drava

Budapest

Tisza

2 Ukr

3 Ukr

Sava

Danube

South-West

Po

F

Adriatic Sea

15

N

0   100 miles
0   100km

AFTERMATH

Evaluating the siege of Budapest is complex. Contemporary press articles called it a 'Second Stalingrad'. Such a comparison, however, is in many ways false. Hungary was only a secondary theatre of war, and the events taking place here did not have a major influence on the course of the war, whereas Stalingrad was a defining main-theatre event and turning point in World War II. It would also be wrong to draw parallels in regard to casualties. The Battle of Stalingrad witnessed over a million casualties, whereas Budapest had fewer than 100,000 from all sides.

Between October 1944 and 13 February 1945, the 2nd and 3rd Ukrainian fronts suffered losses of 320,000 dead, wounded or missing, but this number is for the whole area covered by the two fronts, and only a part of these can be attributed to Budapest. We only have estimates for Soviet casualties, as accurate data does not exist or is not yet available. In the course of the *Konrad* relief operations, the Soviets lost an estimated 60,000 troops and about 900 tanks and assault guns, while the Germans lost about 21,000 troops and about 300 tanks and assault guns.

In the battles within Budapest's perimeter, essentially all defending forces were lost, except for the 785 troops who successfully broke out, and the 1,476 troops evacuated through the air bridge. Of the 3,074 missions flown by the Budapest Supply Staff, 2,467 were successful, and 38 Ju 52s, 14 He 111s and 11 DFS 230s were shot down. A total of 1,953 tons of supplies (1,707 tons of ammunition, 118 tons of fuel and 128 tons of food) were delivered. Soviet casualties within the city fall somewhere between the extreme estimates of 30,000 to 100,000 troops. It is clear the Soviets suffered more casualties during the German relief attempts than in Budapest. The Romanians suffered 5,500 casualties in the Budapest fighting, but between their crossing of the Tisza and their withdrawal from Budapest, they lost more than 10,000 troops.

A Hungarian civilian offers food to a German infantryman. By the end of the siege, both soldiers and civilians were starving. (Süddeutsche Zeitung/Alamy)

Among the city's Hungarian civilian population, the number of dead lies somewhere between 25,000–30,000 people, many of which are confirmed by the death registries. Overall, the losses in Budapest are far below those of Stalingrad. The buildings in the inner parts of the city, mainly in Buda Castle and its surroundings, suffered severe damage, but in general, the buildings in most of the city remained intact or only slightly damaged. Only 4.6 per cent of housing was destroyed.

Why, then, did the contemporary press tag the siege as a 'Second Stalingrad'? The reason is that in some places and for short periods, the intensity of fighting indeed was comparable to that of the Battle of Stalingrad. Another reason is that this battle also took place in a large city. However, it needs to be emphasized that any intensive fighting was limited to very short periods and to restricted locations in the city, whereas in the rest of the city, there was often complete calm for even weeks at a time.

In evaluating the siege of Budapest, we must look at the broader context. All through the campaign, the Soviet command focused on capturing the city, which did not inflict a serious blow on the Germans in either economic or political terms. Compared to Germany's military industry, Budapest's industrial capacities were negligible. In terms of politics and the pro-German Szálasi government, the loss of Budapest did not cause problems, nor was it in any way a turning point as regards military resistance. In contrast, the Soviets did not recognize the economic significance of the Transdanubia region for the Germans, and the Germans did indeed control parts of the region and its raw material resources up until March 1945.

The plans drawn up by the Soviets to capture Budapest were too ambitious, and would only have worked (even partially) using surprise. Outside Budapest, where the Germans were already anticipating the attack and still had sufficient reserves available, the Soviet attempts failed. The Soviet efforts to encircle the Hungarian capital eventually succeeded, but instead of a quick and easy victory, a lengthy urban struggle ensued, for which the Soviets lacked manpower. Also, the Soviet air forces and air defences failed to cut the air bridge, which was key for the Germans in holding the Budapest pocket, allowing supplies to be delivered to the end.

Though the Germans continually lost territory to Soviet attacks, they managed to hold Budapest throughout 1944. Yet, they could not prevent the city being surrounded. In the *Konrad* operations, the Germans had their greatest successes when they attacked in places and at times the Soviets were not expecting. Surprise and speed were key. At the same time, the Germans also suffered from insufficient manpower, in both the *Konrad* operations and the defence of Budapest. In the former, there was not enough infantry available to exploit success, such as neutralizing surrounded Soviet divisions or eliminating AT zones. They also lacked experienced soldiers for the defence of Budapest, relying instead on SS cavalry, tankers and Volks-grenadiers; only the Hungarians had infantry available.

Together, the siege of Budapest and the German relief attempts tied down the 2nd and 3rd Ukrainian fronts for months. It took more than 50 days of urban combat to capture the capital, and moreover some of the Axis troops that broke out managed to reach friendly lines. Considering the targets set by the Soviets in autumn 1944, this was hardly an overwhelming success and did little to change the course of the war. Parts of Transdanubia remained under German control for nearly two more months. By comparison, in the time it took to capture Budapest, the Red Army advanced from Warsaw to near Berlin (although the balance of forces here was quite different). For the Axis side, although more than 2,000 troops got out (some evacuated via the air bridge, and some in the breakout), this was little consolation compared to the lost divisions.

From a Hungarian perspective, the siege of Budapest is significant not only for its military aspects, but also for its direct and indirect consequences. The population of the Hungarian capital was not prepared for urban fighting lasting several months. Although life carried on in the siege, it became increasingly difficult to obtain food, and people starved in huge numbers. The situation was aggravated by the fact that Budapest had the last ghetto in Europe into which, by the end of the siege, nearly 70,000 people were crowded. The civilians living in shelters were constantly harassed by police, gendarmes and Arrow Cross raids, seeking Jews hiding outside the ghetto, and men of the proper age to levy for military service. The latter were sent to the front line as reinforcements, but they had no real combat value and deserted as soon as they could.

Civilian life improved little as the front moved on. Supply conditions remained unchanged, and Soviet troops continued to pilfer the city for a long time. Men were now not levied but captured as prisoners of war. The Soviets also took some Jews liberated from the ghetto as prisoners of war. About 90,000 civilians, not only men but also women, were deported from Budapest and the surrounding towns to prison camps. Many of them never returned from the Soviet Union, and even those who returned were often broken by the experience.

For women, individual and gang rape was a fact of life on a mass scale during the siege and in the months that followed. The number of victims is easily in the tens of thousands, or even 100,000. The situation was so severe that for the first time in the history of Hungary, the ban on abortion was lifted.

The food supply situation improved little even after the fighting ended, as feeding the populace was not a primary concern for the Soviets. At the same time, Hungary had to surrender a huge portion of its agricultural produce to the Red Army. Even in March and April 1945, the population of Budapest was threatened by food shortages. Some starved to death in the city under Soviet control.

The mass pilfering by Soviet and Romanian troops was a minor nuisance compared to the above evils. The pilferers took not only valuables but also food from an already destitute population. The situation was slow to improve, and public security was far from good even a year after the siege.

The siege of Budapest remained a painful memory for the people living through it. Moreover, in the communist years that followed, the survivors could not freely talk about what happened after the siege, and this was also left out of official histories, remaining only as personal memories and family stories until the transition to democracy in 1989.

Most of Budapest's citizens did not see the end of the siege as liberation, and despite all the subsequent propaganda, the grievances they suffered were not forgotten. Nor did the Red Army see it as such; unlike for Warsaw, Vienna and Belgrade, the commemorative medals awarded for taking part in the fighting refer to 'capturing' the city, not liberating it. All this says a lot about what the Soviets themselves thought of the issue.

BIBLIOGRAPHY

The Liberty Statue on Gellért Hill, originally erected to the memory of Soviet troops. In 1993 the monument was altered, with the statue of a Soviet soldier taken down and the inscription changed to remove mention of the 'liberating Soviet heroes'. The removed Soviet soldier, together with other statues (including those of captains Steinmetz and Ostapenko), was relocated to Memento Park in Kamaerdő. (Author's collection)

Balázs, Sándor, Dr. Újj, Írisz, *Óbuda ostroma 1944–1945*, Óbudai Múzeuum, Budapest, 2005

Gosztonyi, Péter, *Budapest lángokban 1944–1945*, Móra Ferenc Könyvkiadó, Budapest, 1998

Gosztonyi, Péter, *Der Kampf um Budapest*, Verlag Schnell & Steiner, München, 1964

Gosztonyi, Péter, *Endkampf an der Donau: 1944/45*, Wien-München-Zürich, Fritz Molden, 1969

Harrison, Richard, *The Budapest Operation: An Operational-Strategic Study*, Solihull, Helion and Company, 2017

Hingyi, László, *Budapest ostroma 1944–1945 I–III: Források Budapest ostromának történetéből (The Siege of Budapest, 1944–1945, I–III: Sources from the History of the Siege of Budapest)*, Budapest, Etalon, 2018–2020

Maier, Georg, *Drama Between Budapest and Vienna: The Final Fighting of the 6th Panzer-Armee in the East – 1945*, Winnipeg, J.J. Fedorowicz Publishing, 2004

Markó, György, *Az elsodort város: Emlékkötet a Budapestért folytatott harcok 60. évfordulójára 1944/45 (A Swept-away City: A Collection Commemorating the 60th Anniversary of the Fighting for Budapest 1944/45)*, Budapest, PolgArt, 2005

Mihályi, Balázs, *Dél-Buda ostroma 1944–1945 (The Siege of Southern Buda, 1944–1945)*, Budapest, np, 2011

Mihályi, Balázs, *Budapest Battlefield Guide 1944–1945*, Budapest, np, 2011

Mihályi, Balázs, *Honvédek és hungaristák a Budapest erődben 1944–1945 (Defenders and Hungarists in Budapest Fortress, 1944–1945)*, Budapest, Erődítés Történeti Egyesület, 2018

Mihályi, Balázs, *Emlékek Budapest ostromáról, a kitörésről és a hadifogságról 1944–1945 (Memories of the Siege of Budapest, the Breakout and the Prison Camps, 1944–1945)*, Budapest, Erődítés Történeti Egyesület, 2019

Mihályi, Balázs, *Budapest ostroma: A polgári áldozatok (The Siege of Budapest: Civilian Casualties)*, Kárpátia Stúdió, 2020

Mihályi, Balázs, Tulok, Péter and Tóth, Gábor, *A Várnegyed ostroma: Buda 1944–45*, Budapest, Budavári Önkormányzat-Litea Könyvesbolt, 2018

Nevenkin, Kamen, *Take Budapest!: The Struggle for Hungary Autumn 1944*, Stroud, The History Press, 2013

Nevenkin, Kamen, *Fortress Budapest 1–2: The Siege of the Hungarian Capital 1944–45*, Gyömrő, Peko, 2020

Számvéber, Norbert, *The Sword Behind the Shield: A Combat History of the German Efforts to Relieve Budapest 1945 – Operation 'Konrad' I, III, III*, Solihull, Helion and Company, 2016

Tucker-Jones, Anthony, *The Battle for Budapest 1944–1945: Rare Photographs from Wartime Archives*, South Yorkshire, Pen and Sword Military, 2016

Ungváry, Krisztián, *The Battle for Budapest: 100 Days in World War II*, London, I. B. Tauris, 2003

THE BATTLEFIELD TODAY

In Budapest, Buda Castle is a popular tourist site. Here, on Dísz Square, a single storey of the former Army High Command building is still visible. Not far from the castle, the Hospital in the Rock Nuclear Bunker Museum is in Lovas Street – an exhibition there has several rooms dedicated to World War II events. Near Mary Magdalene Church, missing its tower, lies the Military History Institute and Museum. The Citadella fortress on top of Gellért Hill is currently under restoration. On the Pest bank, the House of Terror Museum on Andrássy Avenue includes a section on the events of 1944–45. Also in Pest, the Holocaust Memorial Centre on Páva Street holds displays on the siege of the capital.

INDEX

Figures in **bold** refer to illustrations and their captions.